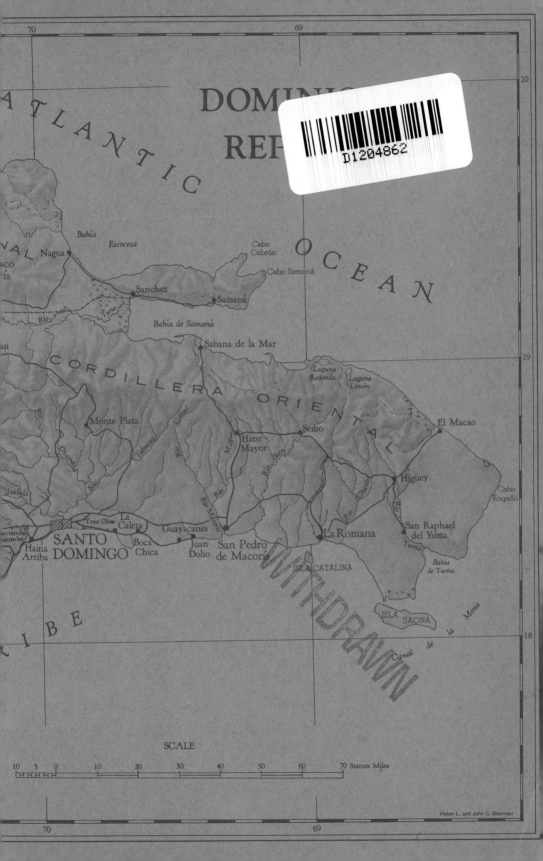

DOMINIC[AN]

REP[UBLIC]

ATLANTIC

OCEAN

Bahía Escocesa

Nagua

Cabo Cabrón

Cabo Samaná

Sanchez

Samaná

Bahía de Samaná

Sabana de la Mar

CORDILLERA ORIENTAL

Laguna Redonda

Laguna Limón

Monte Plata

El Macao

Seibo

Hato Mayor

Higüey

Cabo Engaño

Isabela

Tres Ojos

La Caleta

Guayacanes

San Raphael del Yuma

SANTO DOMINGO

Boca Chica

Juan Dolio

San Pedro de Macoris

La Romana

Bahía de Yuma

Haina Arriba

Hacienda

gombe

ISLA CATALINA

ISLA SAONA

Canal de la Mona

RIBE

SCALE

10 5 0   10   20   30   40   50   60   70 Statute Miles

Helen L. and John C. Sherman

Quisqueya

A HISTORY OF THE DOMINICAN REPUBLIC

" 'Two revolutions ago,' the old Dominican lady said, 'my son took a gun and went into politics.' "

—*Otto Schoenrich, 1918*

"That people which views the exercise of its own rights with indifference, is preparing itself to become enslaved."

—*Ulises Espaillat, 1876*

Quisqueya

A HISTORY OF THE DOMINICAN REPUBLIC

by Selden Rodman

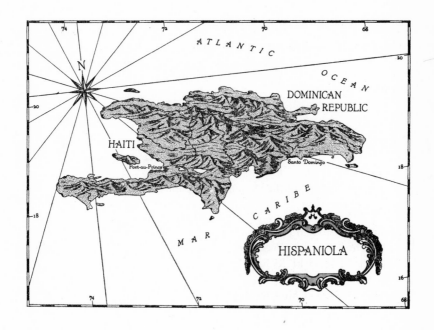

1964

UNIVERSITY OF WASHINGTON PRESS · SEATTLE

BOOKS BY SELDEN RODMAN

VERSE

Death of the Hero
The Amazing Year
The Revolutionists
The Airmen
Lawrence: The Last Crusade
Mortal Triumph and Other Poems

ART

Rangefinders: The Artist as Nonconformist
The Insiders
Conversations with Artists
The Eye of Man
Portrait of the Artist as an American
Renaissance in Haiti
Horace Pippin: A Negro Artist in America

MUSIC

The Heart of Beethoven

TRAVEL

Mexican Journal: The Conquerors Conquered
Haiti: The Black Republic

HISTORY

Quisqueya: A History of the Dominican Republic

ANTHOLOGIES

One Hundred Modern Poems
One Hundred American Poems
War and the Poet (with Richard Eberhart)
The Poetry of Flight
A New Anthology of Modern Poetry

Copyright © 1964 by the University of Washington Press
Library of Congress Catalog Card Number 64-17389
Manufactured by the George Banta Company, Inc., Menasha, Wisconsin
Designed by Adrian Wilson

Preface

During the years I visited and lived in Haiti—writing about its indomitable people, initiating its mural-painting "renaissance," exploring every corner of that magnificent (and roadless) terrain—the idea grew in the back of my head to some day get to know the eastern part of Hispaniola as well. But in those years (1940-60) it could not be done—except on Trujillo's terms. The roads were great, but in every other sense this state was as inaccessible as Tibet or the moon. I made three trips of reconnaissance across the border. On the last, in 1949, my views of the dictatorship had become sufficiently well known abroad to gain me the honor of a visit from the secret police and an order to leave the country within twenty-four hours. It was then that I determined to come back as soon as Trujillo should be overthrown and to write the first complete history of the Dominican Republic.

I flew to Santo Domingo during the crucial winter of 1962, when the newly installed Council of State was expecting a return of the assassinated dictator's brothers, and had a talk at the National Palace with Vice President Donald Reid Cabral. He showed me under his desk the submachine gun he then felt obliged to carry at all times, and he assured me that only his death and that of the other councillors would prevent the holding of free elections in December. That month I returned, and in the winter that followed I took the notes on which the final chapters and appendix of this book are substantially based.

v

My bibliography is misleading in one respect. Ninety per cent of the books included in it are short on facts; few of them contributed more than a sentence, a date, a fleeting insight. The exceptions, to which anyone writing on the Dominican Republic must be indebted, are the following five books:

Samuel Eliot Morison, *Admiral of the Ocean Sea: A Life of Christopher Columbus* (Boston, Little, Brown, 1942).
M. L. E. Moreau de St.-Mery, *A Topographical and Political Description of the Spanish Part of Santo-Domingo,* trans. William Cobbett (Philadelphia, Printed by the author, 1796).
Sumner Welles, *Naboth's Vineyard: The Dominican Republic 1844-1924* (New York, Payson Clarke, Ltd., 1928).
Otto Schoenrich, *Santo Domingo: A Country with a Future* (New York, Macmillan, 1918).
Germán E. Ornes, *Trujillo: Little Caesar of the Caribbean* (New York, Thomas Nelson, 1958).

The first, as everyone knows, is a flawlessly documented and superbly written account of Columbus' voyages. Moreau de St.-Mery's eighteenth-century travelogue, while inferior to his companion volume on Haiti and not unprejudiced, is surprisingly modern in its scientific spirit. Welles's two-volume history of the period from the Independence of 1844 to the withdrawal of the American marines in 1924, is exhaustive and eloquent; its two flaws—a racial prejudice directed principally at Haitians and a tendency to hero-worship Horacio Vásquez—detract little from its Olympian authority. Schoenrich's book contains a serviceable historical summary of the events up to 1914 and some good chapters on topography, botany, and local customs. Ornes' polemic against Trujillo, written in 1958, contains a wealth of detail on the family relations, politics, and mythology of the dictatorship. Since four of these five books have long been out of print (Morison's is available), part of my endeavor has been to include in this narrative as much as possible of what is still relevant and interesting in theirs. But three other primary sources deserve special mention: Leyburn's social study of the Haitian people; Balaguer's sketchy life of Duarte, because it happens to be the only one; and Palm's impeccable little pamphlet describing the historical monuments of the capital.

Friends in the Dominican Republic who were most helpful with their companionship, historical knowledge or advice, and who will accept my gratitude without being necessarily committed to any of my conclusions, were: Donald Reid Cabral; Buenaventura Sánchez, Minister of Education in the Bosch Government; Malcolm McLean, Cultural Affairs Officer with the United States Information Agency; Tomás A. Pastoriza; Alejandro Mencía; Federico García-Godoy; Tom Stocker; and Dan Perlmutter.

Also: Kurt Bachman, Lloyd Gaspar, Thayer Waldo, Norman Ward, Julio Senior, Humberto Soto-Ricart, Angel Miolán, Germán Ornes, Emile de Boyrie Moya, Bruno Philip, Maia Rodman, Lorenzo Berry, Robert B. Sandin, Gregory and Patricia Simms, Gustavo Tavares E., Colonel Robert D. Heinl, Jr., James Caesar Browning, Major Howard Cleveland, Raymond L. Thurston, American Ambassador to Haiti in 1962-63, Marian and Clark Blyth, Emilio Rodríguez Demorizi, General Antonio Imbert, Puro Gómez, Pedro Antonio Ramos Rodríguez, Ferain Antonio Almonte, James Finley, Crandall Spence, Maximo Pou, Bishop Paul Kellogg, Rev. James A. Douglass, Prospero Mella Chavvíer, Gary and Clover Burke.

Far more than for the incidental help she gave me in researching and typing parts of this manuscript, and reading all of it, I owe to my wife Carole the fact that all of the year involved was spent in health and perfect happiness.

September, 1963
Oakland, N.J.

Contents

Quisqueya

A HISTORY OF THE DOMINICAN REPUBLIC

Paradise Lost, 1492-1533

From the Coming of Columbus to the Extinction of the Indians

On the afternoon of February 5, 1492, the island of Hispaniola, second largest of the Caribbean and twenty-fourth in the world, had never been seen except by the eyes of its aboriginal inhabitants. That night Christopher Columbus, guiding his flagship *Santa Maria* across the Windward Passage from Cuba, sighted the land his Indian guides had already described to him as "Bohío" or "Haïti" and came to anchor, along with *Niña*, in the harbor of Môle St. Nicholas.

The great Italian explorer, who had already described Cuba to his Spanish masters as unparalleled "in fertility, in mildness of cold and heat, in abundance of good and pure water," was about to find these blessings and much more in the big island he soon named, out of his joyful gratitude, for Spain itself. For had the natives of Hispaniola in their innocence not brought to Columbus abundant amulets and masques of pure gold, the chances are that the Admiral's first voyage would have been written off by Ferdinand and Isabella of Castile as a costly failure. As it was, Columbus found not only evidence of the riches the practical king had envisioned as transforming Spain in a matter of decades into the world's most powerful empire. He found also the millions of "uncommitted souls" whose conversion to Christianity, by fire and sword if need be, the gentle queen had recommended as "the end and the beginning" of Columbus' whole enterprise. The tragic history of Spanish America was ready to be written, as it would be throughout the five centuries to follow, in blood.

On January 4 of the new year Columbus was to sight Monte Cristi, the northwesternmost elevation of that part of the island the Indians called Quisqueya—now the Dominican Republic. The events of the five preceding weeks had been fateful. For one thing, the sailors had captured an Indian girl whose only adornment was a golden noseplug; it was a token that this island promised more than Cuba. On December 16, near the site of the present Haitian village of Port-de-Paix, the Spaniards had been welcomed by several hundred natives and engaged in trade for gold with glass beads and other trinkets. Columbus received a young *cacique* (chief) aboard with the equivalent of a twenty-one-gun salute, but in his journal he revealed his real intentions toward the Indians: "They bear no arms, and are all unprotected and so very cowardly that a thousand would not face three; so they are fit to be ordered about and made to work. . . ." Commenting on these words some years later when the enslavement of the Indians was a fact and their extinction imminent, the benevolent priest Bartolomé de Las Casas had this to say:

> Note here, that the natural, simple and kind gentleness and humble condition of the Indians, and want of protection, gave the Spaniards the insolence to hold them of little account, and to impose on them the harshest tasks that they could, and to become glutted with oppression and destruction. And sure it is that here the Admiral enlarged himself in speech more than he should, and that what he here conceived and set forth from his lips, was the beginning of the ill usage he afterwards inflicted upon them.

Sailing eastward in search of the sources of the gold he had now seen, the Admiral met his first real setback in the New World on a coral reef just past Cap Haïtien. On Christmas Day his flagship *Santa Maria* ran aground. As she broke up slowly under the pounding of the surf, her cargo and gear were taken ashore by Indian porters supplied by a friendly *cacique,* Guacanagarí, and Columbus recorded with evident surprise that not so much as a board or a nail was stolen. The following day the *cacique* came aboard *Niña* "and almost weeping said that he must not show grief, that he would give him [Columbus] all he had, and that he had given the Christians who were ashore two very big houses, and would give them more if necessary." To such an extent, Columbus added, were they "loyal and without greed for the property of others." If the Admiral was struck by the irony of it all when Guacanagarí then presented him with a great mask having eyes and ears of gold, he did not show it.

After leaving a colony of thirty-nine men at Navidad, where *Santa Maria* had foundered, Columbus sailed on to Monte Cristi. Windbound there two weeks, he spent the time exploring the mouth of the Rio Yaque del Norte and reported its sands to be full of gold grains, some as big as lentils. *Pinta* meanwhile had rejoined him, and on January 9 the two ships looked in to the fine harbor of Puerto Plata. Three days later, anchored in twelve fathoms off Samaná Bay, the expedition encountered the first apparently hostile Indians.

These were not Tainos (Arawaks), like all they had so far met with, but Caribs, a marauding cannibal people who had worked their way up the Lesser Antillean chain from South America. They had just begun to overrun Puerto Rico and were presently preying on the peaceful Tainos of eastern Hispaniola. The Tainos, for their part, had earlier pushed westward a more primitive people, the Siboneys, a last remnant of which Columbus was to meet with in western Cuba. It is significant that remnants of the Caribs survive to this day, but no Tainos. The moment Columbus first encountered these small-boned, pastoral, peaceable Indians in the Bahamas, he noted their frail fish-tooth spears and confided to his journal that they would be pushovers. The very word for the Tainos' language group, Arawak, means meal- or cassava-eater. The Tainos were expert basket weavers and made masterly sculpture and ceramics, but this was not noticed until centuries after they had been obliterated. The fact that the Caribs had managed to arm themselves with bows and arrows, and had no inhibitions about using them on strangers, counted for more in the race to keep up with Western civilization.

The Caribs Columbus now encountered did not actually attack the Spaniards, but when they turned suddenly toward a pile of weapons from which they had been bartering specimens with the seamen, Columbus' men fell upon them, wounding two and routing the rest.

Two days later *Pinta* and *Niña* set sail for Spain.

Columbus' second expedition to the New World took off from Cadiz September 25, 1493. This time, encouraged by the samplings of gold and Indians the Admiral had brought back with him, the sovereigns made a substantial investment. There were seventeen vessels and fifteen hundred men and the Admiral was given to understand that although he should continue to treat the Indians "lovingly," he must this time convert them to Christianity. To accomplish this mission there accompanied him one Fray Boil (or Buil) "with other *religiosos.*" The other purpose of the expedition, collecting gold, was played down in Columbus' instructions.

The crossing was made in thirty-nine days. First touching at Guadaloupe, the fleet raided several Carib settlements, enjoyed its first taste of pineapple and sweet potato, and—apparently foregoing "conversion" for later on—carried off "twelve very beautiful and plump girls from 15 to 16 years old." At St. Croix in the Virgins, making another foray in search of girls and boys, the sailors had their first armed encounter with the natives, besting them in an unequal battle and carrying off more slaves. Puerto Rico's southern coast was discovered November 18 or 19; sailing through the Mona Passage, the fleet took on provisions and water at the eastern tip of Hispaniola and began to proceed cautiously westward along the north coast toward Monte Cristi and the colony of shipmates left at Navidad the Christmas before.

Columbus' subsequent treatment of the Indians has been explained, if not justified, on the grounds that the massacre of his first colonists demanded retaliatory measures. The truth of the matter, shortly discovered, was that the "colonists" had soon split into gangs, roving the interior in search of gold and women. Guacanagarí tolerated them, but Caonabo of Maguana, a sterner *cacique,* put those he caught to death. Descending upon Navidad, where he found the rest of the Spaniards living with five captured women apiece and no guard, he drove them into the sea. When Guacanagarí protested truthfully to Columbus that he had tried to stop Caonabo and had come to the aid of the fleeing remnant of the Europeans, Father Boil demanded that he be pronounced guilty without trial and executed. Columbus, more humane, spared him. But the rank and file of Spaniards determined to take their revenge in good time.

Now was made a decision, seemingly of little consequence at the time, which was destined to affect the future of the incredibly rich island and insure its division. With Navidad gone, where to establish the permanent settlement? A very few miles to the west of Caracol Bay, with a high, dry, and healthy harbor base amid superb planting lands, lay the site of the future city of Cap Haïtien, two hundred years later to be built by the French into the "Paris of the Antilles," capital of the world's richest colony. But the Spaniards, profoundly repelled by the idea of actually working for wealth, had heard from the Tainos that the great central valley to the east, which they called Cibao, was the source of gold. Beating against the prevailing trade winds at the rate of thirty-two miles in twenty-five days —"more trouble," as the ships' doctor put it, "than to come all the way from Castile"—the fleet anchored January 2, 1494, at one of the least promising roadsteads in the whole coastline and proceeded to build the ill-fated settlement of Isabela.

Today nothing remains of that "city" on the lea of the cape between Monte Cristi and Puerto Plata but a few vine-covered stones. Even the poorest peasants today have found better places to establish their grass or adobe huts. But for two more years, until the building of Santo Domingo on the south coast began in 1496, Isabela, jerry-built and disease ridden, was to be the early fulcrum of the most ruthless pursuit of gold in the world's history.

Following the first Mass celebrated in the New World, the initial expedition into the Cibao set forth. It was under the leadership of Alonso de Hojeda, described ambiguously by Las Casas as "very devoted to Our Lady" and "always the first to draw blood whenever there was a war or a quarrel." Gold nuggets sent back to Isabela were so weighty that Columbus endeavored to put off the clamor for return to Spain until they should have a measurable cargo. But the homesick men would not wait. They demanded edible (meaning European) food. Early in February twelve of the seventeen vessels set sail, carrying 30,000 ducats' worth of gold, sixty parrots, and scores of slaves, most of whom died on the voyage.

Columbus, meanwhile, mounted his own voyage into the interior. At the ravine called Paso de los Hidalgos (Gate of the Gentlemen) there came for the first time into view that part of the Cibao known to this day by the appropriate name he gave it, the Vega Real. Whether this "Royal Plain" was then graced as it is now by stands of *madre de cacao* trees whose pink blossoms stand out like coral islands in that incredible expanse of sea-green fertility, Las Casas was soon to describe it as "a place that ought to call forth blessings and infinite thanks to the Creator." It was, he added, a place of "such perfection, grace and beauty that they who saw it thought they had arrived in some part of paradise." As the conquistadors marched through this great garden to the Rio Yaque del Norte at the present site of Santiago, the Dominican Republic's second city, they were showered with presents. But the Indians ("imbued with all the virtues," Las Casas sadly relates) could not understand why the Spaniards restrained them from helping themselves in turn to bits of the soldiers' decorative equipment. Crossing the river on the backs of these Indians, Columbus built his first fortress, Santo Tomás, near the present village of Jánico, collecting at the same time bushels of gold nuggets from his generous hosts. The way back took twenty-nine days amid "terrible weather, bad food and worse drink," but it was made bearable, according to one of the Spaniards, by "covetousness for that gold" which kept them all "strong and lusty."

Peace with the Indians was broken during the second expedition out of Isabela, April 9, 1494. Hojeda, hearing that clothing had been stolen during one of the crossings of the Yaque, cut off the ears of one of the local chieftain's men and sent the chieftain with his brother and nephew in chains to Isabela. Only the tears of a *cacique* whose loyalty he counted on kept the Admiral from beheading them in the plaza. "This," says Las Casas of Hojeda's crime, "was the first injustice, with vain and erroneous pretension of doing justice, that was committed in these Indies against the Indians, and the beginning of the shedding of blood, which has since flowed so copiously in this island."

The first crops—imported melons, wheat, and sugar-cane—were now beginning to be harvested at Isabela, but morale was low. On April 24, leaving his brother Diego and Fray Boil in charge, Columbus set forth in three caravels for the exploration of southern Cuba and Jamaica.

Leaving Jamaica on August 9, 1494, Columbus sighted the south peninsula of Haiti August 20. Coasting westward toward the Bay of Jacmel, he was sure that this was indeed Hispaniola again when an Indian in a canoe paddled alongside one of the caravels and shouted "Almirante! Almirante!" By the end of the month the Admiral had discovered Alta Vela rock, the island's southernmost point, and six days later the mouth of Rio Haina in Santo Domingo Bay, whence couriers were dispatched northward to the colony at Isabela. Continuing eastward along the hitherto unexplored southern coast, Columbus discovered Saona Island—the Dominican Republic's largest outlying possession, now barren, but then apparently fertile and densely populated, according to Michel de Cuneo of Savona to whom Columbus presented it as a gift and who promptly erected upon it a cross and a gallows in the name of His Majesty the King. Diverting his course from Cape Engaño to obtain Carib slaves for shipment home in lieu of gold, Columbus developed a high fever and other symptoms which his biographer, Morison, equates with the modern nervous breakdown. A fleet council decided to abandon the foray into Puerto Rico. On September 29 Columbus was carried ashore at Isabela.

Morison titled his chapter on the next phase of Columbus' colonial enterprise "Hell on Hispaniola," and the phrase contains no exaggeration. The chapter begins with the following account of what Columbus' two lieutenants had been doing while the Admiral was away:

> While Hojeda held the fort of Santo Tomás, Margarit and his merry men roved the Vega Real, extorting gold from the natives, raping their women and quickly exhausting their food supplies. The Indians never kept much food on hand in a country of such natural bounty; and, as Las Casas said without much exaggeration, "one Spaniard ate more in a day than a whole family of natives would consume in a month." When the natives refused to furnish what they had not, Margarit's men resorted to threats and blows and whippings, "not only against the common people, but the noble and chief men who were called *nitaynos*"; they carried off many wives and daughters "with no respect to person or dignity, or marriage relation," and kidnaped young boys to serve them as slaves.

The outbreak that followed has been called by one historian "the first Dominican revolution." Taken to task by Diego and Bartholomew Columbus, Margarit marched on Isabela, where he was joined in mutiny by Father Boil—who had yet to convert his first Indian. Seizing Bartholomew's three caravels, they sailed for Spain where they proceeded to malign Columbus and ridicule the potential of Hispaniola.

It is astonishing that Columbus, returning to Isabela at this junc-

ture, profited nothing by the experience. Had he denounced the out-
laws, he would have had allies, thousands of them, when he needed
them later. It was his last chance and he lost it. Not only did he fail
to arraign the bands of soldiers still terrorizing the natives in the
interior; he turned on their innocent victims, hunting them on horse-
back with dogs, rounding up fifteen hundred Tainos as captives and
shipping five hundred of them ("the best males and females") to
Spain as slaves. And this in the face of his sovereigns' coldness to a
milder proposition he had earlier made to them: to enslave the war-
like Caribs only.

The Tainos, for their part, did not have to be informed that most
of their captured brethren perished before reaching the slave market;
what was happening to them in their own land was terrible enough
to make the Tainos take thought for survival by any means. But it
was already too late. Like Montezuma in Mexico twenty-five years
later, Guacanagarí had made the mistake of believing that friendli-
ness, generosity, and loyalty would be rewarded by a display of
similar virtues on the part of his Christian guests. And just as Cortés
by lies and unlimited terrorism had managed to set tribe against
tribe before the Aztecs could come to their senses and had then captured the tardy direct-actionist Cuauthémoc by treachery and hanged
him, so Alonso de Hojeda, reversing the procedure, was able to defeat the hosts of Guatiguaná, using the loyal Guacanagarí as an ally,
and then lure the fierce Caonabo himself into ambush with false
promises, and handcuff him to the wall of Isabela's crowded jail.

The decisive battle in which the Indians were routed took place
at the present site of the ruins of Fort Concepción de la Vega on
March 27, 1495. Spanish historians allege that the Indians num-
bered one hundred thousand, Columbus' men two hundred. As with
Cortés, horses played a decisive role, the superstitious Indians at first
assuming that rider and mount were one. A legend, for which there
is no historical foundation, has it that as the battle reached its climax,
with the issue in doubt, the Virgin of Las Mercedes appeared on an
arm of the wooden cross carried by one of the soldiers. This appari-

tion, according to the Catholics, so unnerved the Indians that they dropped their arms and fled in terror. The place where the cross was supposed to have been planted is still shown to visitors under the floor of the Santo Cerro church outside La Vega.

Hispaniola was pacified. Which is to say that it would never know real peace again. By 1496 the Indians had been so thoroughly intimidated that the king was able to boast that a single Spaniard in Hispaniola could go where he pleased, enjoying free food, women, and pickaback rides. To supplement the white population, now reduced to 630, Columbus was preparing to sail for Spain when a hurricane—an act of divine retribution, in Las Casas' view—destroyed his ships. While rebuilding them, he devised an ingenious means of making the Indians pay for their own pacification. It was a system "irrational," "impossible," "intolerable," and "abominable" in Las Casas' words, and its consequence was to be the total extinction of the native population, with an alternative "solution" of the labor problem for which the West is still paying an incalculable price. But in terms of immediate material gain it worked. Every Indian on the island, in lieu of death, was to furnish four times annually a Flanders hawk's bell full of gold dust. Since the available supply of gold in the riverbeds was fast vanishing, and since most Indians lived far from the Cibao where gold was still to be found, twenty-five pounds of spun or woven cotton was declared an acceptable substitute for gold.

Most Indians were quite incapable of supplying either. One desperate *cacique* offered a rational alternative: set aside a tract of arable land and the Indians would grow wheat enough, in Las Casas' estimate, to feed the whole kingdom of Castile ten times over. Columbus would have none of it. "Christian and virtuous as he was, and full of good desires," Las Casas says, the Admiral was too anxious to stop the mouths of his critics with gold to do more than reduce the tribute. Yet far from even supporting their few mouths with the abundance of fruit and grain that could be harvested from the blackest, deepest loam on earth, these "colonists" began importing their essential foods—an economic absurdity that persists in Hispaniola to this day.

The Indians were still unable to pay the reduced tribute. "Then straightway against them," Las Casas says, "was taken the vengeance which the Christians call punishment." Some fled to the high mountains, pursued by hounds. Others were captured and horribly mutilated. Thousands took cassava poison. More thousands died of disease and starvation. Of the indigenous population of the island, estimated to have been as high as three million in 1492, and no lower than three hundred thousand, one third was killed off by 1496. A census of 1508 revealed only sixty thousand survivors. And by 1548 Fernandez de Oviedo, the Spanish colonial historian, doubted that five hundred Tainos remained.

At daybreak on March 10, 1496, a tiny remnant of the seventeen proud ships with which Columbus had hopefully set forth three years before, sailed for Spain with 225 Christians and 30 Indians aboard. Among the latter was Caonabo who died at sea. Three months later the bedraggled survivors entered Cadiz Bay.

The story of Columbus' third and fourth voyages to Hispaniola is soon told and without significant new consequences, but the last stand of the Indians offers an heroic footnote to the otherwise pathetic history of native subjugation.

The third voyage began with six caravels setting sail from the port of Seville May 30, 1498. Instructions this time reiterated that priests were to be taken along and encouraged to get on with the business of "converting the Indians of the said Indies to our Holy Catholic Faith." Pardons were offered to criminals in the Spanish jails if they would enlist as colonists. Columbus was empowered to allot land to individuals in Hispaniola, reserving only gold and logwood to the Crown.

After discovering Trinidad and the coastline of Venezuela, Columbus' fleet dropped anchor in the Ozama River, the port of Santo

Domingo, on August 31. Brother Bartholomew, recently commissioned Adelantado of the Indies, was having his troubles. He had dispatched three hundred Indians as slaves to Spain, and he had made some progress building the new capital, Isabela Nueva as it was then called, on the eastern bank of the Ozama, but rebellion had broken out again. This time the offender was a demagogue named Francisco Roldán, and Bartholomew was barely holding him at bay in the fort which the Admiral had built at Concepción de la Vega. With news of Columbus' return, Roldán fled to the fastnesses of his Indian friends in the western mountains of Xaragua, while Guarionex, his native ally in the east, was hunted down and captured after much bloodletting in the Samaná Peninsula. Thirty per cent of the Spaniards still on the island were ill with syphilis, a disease endemic to the Indians which they are thought to have introduced into Europe in unconscious repayment of their debt to Western civilization.

The aging and now arthritic Admiral failed to deal sternly with the mutineers. Not only did he promise Roldán's soldiers free passage home with all their gold and slaves; to pacify the remaining rebels, he devised a system of exploitative land tenure that has plagued Latin America ever since. The *encomiendas* (then known as *repartimientos*) allotted each settler, without obligation to the state, large parcels of Indian land *with the Indians that were on it* in perpetuity. The *caciques,* to get out from under the intolerable gold tribute, agreed to this.

Ferdinand and Isabella, meanwhile, disillusioned by the chaotic conditions in Hispaniola under the three Columbus brothers, appointed Francisco de Bobadilla, a spiteful and arrogant martinet, to sail for the island in 1499 as Royal Commissioner. Arriving in August of 1500, Bobadilla promptly exceeded his authority, and with no respect whatever for the Admiral's genius as a seaman, much less for his relative mildness as a governor, clapped him in irons, together with brothers Diego and Bartholomew, and shipped them home to Spain.

Columbus was released, of course, and even given modest resources to outfit a fourth and final voyage, but not before being given to understand that he was an administrative failure. What must have been his thoughts while witnessing on February 13, 1502, the departure of a new governor of all the Indies, Don Nicolás de Ovando, with a tremendous fleet of thirty vessels and twenty-five hundred men! The Admiral himself was later provided with four small but well-equipped caravels and embarked May 9, 1502 from Cádiz. This time his aim was to discover a strait beyond Cuba and sail home to Spain around the world—an aim somewhat clouded by Columbus' unshakeable conviction that the islands he had already discovered lay off the coast of China, a belief already abandoned by almost every mariner and geographer in Europe.

Arriving before Santo Domingo June 29 to ride out a cyclonic storm he had seen building up, Columbus requested permission to enter the harbor and advised Ovando, whose fleet was preparing to put to sea for the voyage home, to batten down the hatches. Now the great mariner had his revenge. Ovando rejected both messages with insolent disdain. His great fleet sailed into the Mona Passage, carrying Bobadilla, Guarionex, and two hundred thousand *castellanos'* worth of gold, including the greatest nugget ever found in the West Indies. Twenty of the ships were caved in by the wind or smashed to bits on the rocks. Three or four struggled back in a sinking condition. And only one, the very one that happened to be bearing a treasure for Columbus' son Diego, reached Spain. Columbus' squadron, meanwhile, having put in to the mouth of Rio Haina west of the capital, rode out the storm nicely.

The voyage of July 14 to the coast of Honduras and the discomforts suffered by Columbus and his men during the year they were marooned on Jamaica do not concern us here. To avert a scandal, Ovando finally permitted the survivors of the foundered caravels to be brought to Santo Domingo, where Columbus was immediately put aboard a chartered ship for Spain. He arrived there November 7, 1504, and died at Valladolid May 20, 1506.

The story of Enriquillo and his rebellion remains to be told. With it concludes the account of the Indian population of Hispaniola and the unfolding of subsequent Dominican history under two other races.

Even while Columbus had been marooned at Jamaica, Governor Ovando had carried the "pacification" of the native population one step nearer to completion, hanging or burning alive eighty of the recalcitrant *caciques*. One of these, the beautiful Anacaona, queen of the Xaraguas, was invited by Diego Velásquez, the future conqueror of Cuba, to witness a military drill. Receiving the three hundred Spaniards openheartedly, she and her people were watching the spectacle when, at a signal from the trumpets, the Christians turned on their unsuspecting hosts and massacred them. Anacaona was seized and later executed for not being a "sincere" enough Christian.

The King of Spain was well pleased with Ovando. The new governor was sending home increasingly large shipments of gold as Hispaniola began to become the staging area for expeditions into the more golden lands to the west. But in 1509 one of Columbus' wishes was granted posthumously. His son, Don Diego, largely because he had had the good fortune to marry Dona María de Toledo, a cousin of the king, was appointed governor of Hispaniola. Diego Columbus' viceroyalty, divided into two separate "reigns," was not a happy one. He built a splendid palace on the west bank of the Ozama, to which the capital had now been moved. And he brought the pomp of the Castilian court to a provincial city that was already beginning, with its own splendid buildings and ostentatious living, to incite the envy of the sovereign. But the weak Diego was soon caught in a cross fire between the planters, whose maltreatment of the Indians he endeavored to curb, and the various religious orders now vying with each other to protect what was left of the Indians' rights. In 1515 he returned to Spain for five years to try to have his powers strengthened.

To understand what had turned at least some of the Catholic priests away from their original acquiescence in the Indians' fate, it is necessary to describe in some detail the career of the noblest, most complex, and most famous of them, Bartolomé de Las Casas. We have already quoted frequently from his *History of the Indies.* As a young man Las Casas had accompanied Columbus on his third voyage. Four years later he had made the passage again with Ovando. In 1510 he had been admitted to holy orders, the first priest ordained in the American colonies. Participating in the "pacification" of Cuba under Velásquez the following year, he had acquired wealth and many slaves of his own. But very soon after this he seems to have passed through a spiritual crisis or sudden illumination that altered his whole life. He had always been something of a liberal. Now, giving up his worldly possessions, he abruptly became a fanatic and, but for one horrendous error which he was quick to admit and regret, a saint. The subject of Las Casas' fanaticism, which occupied him for the remaining fifty years of his very long life, was the inhumanity and most unchristian treatment of the Indians by his fellow countrymen—a state of affairs which the good bishop did much to alleviate but was powerless to change. His horrendous error, committed in 1517 as the clinching argument in a plea to Charles V to save the Indians from slavery, was to suggest that their liberation be made palatable by giving every Spanish resident in the Americas the right to import twelve Negro slaves. In Las Casas' defense—he himself made none, retiring into a monastery for eight years to expiate his shame—it may be said that slavery was already an established institution in Europe, that Africans in small numbers had already been brought to Hispaniola by Ovando as early as 1503 to work the mines, and that an ecclesiastical point still unresolved was whether a man with black skin could have a "soul."

When Diego Columbus returned to Hispaniola as governor in 1520, he found the Indians being abused by the priests to whom they had been turned over for religious instruction. The planters and mineowners were now using Negro slaves exclusively, and when some of these Africans revolted shortly thereafter, the leaders were hanged. Simultaneously, the last and most effective Indian insurrection had begun. Its leader, Enrique (a cousin of Anacaona), who had been educated and brought up in Christianity by the Spaniards, found himself re-enslaved under the *repartimiento* system. When it became clear to the young man that even his wife must serve the conquerors, he escaped to the Bohoruco Mountains back of Barahona. Rallying a few hundred of the disaffected tribesmen to his standard, Enrique stood off a series of determined efforts to secure his capture.

The story is told, with much sentiment and romantic embellishment, in *Enriquillo,* the classic Dominican novel by Manuel de Jesús Galván. Galván, a secretary to Pedro Santana, the Dominican dictator of the mid-nineteenth century who succeeded briefly in reannexing his country to Spain, was torn between his desire to justify the ways of Spain, and to make a hero worthy of the Rousseauistic cult of the Noble Savage then sweeping libertarian Spanish America. The result is that Galván's Enriquillo is too good to be true. Las Casas is the book's spiritual hero. Enriquillo, trying to please Las Casas and Spain at the same time, must always compromise.

In point of fact, the historical *cacique* did compromise, but only when faced by irresistible force. Diego Columbus had long since retired from the scene in 1533 when Charles V sent Francisco de Barrio-Nuevo after Enriquillo with two hundred of the Emperor's veteran soldiers from Italy. A meeting took place on the island in the salt lake that still bears the young *cacique's* name. On the promise that he and the four thousand remaining Indians in Hispaniola would retire, free but territorially confined, Enriquillo capitulated. For once the Spaniards kept their word. They had nothing to lose. Hardier Negro labor was already carrying the mineral exploitation of Hispaniola into its final decade. By 1540 Santo Domingo had entered its long decline and the Indians, rapidly dying out in their enclosure at Boyá, were forgotten. They would be brought back to life, a Dominican poet was to say, only as "a symbol of patriotism and love of liberty."

II

"*Foolish Spain*," *1534-1785*

The Decay of the Colony through Three Centuries of Imperial Rule

Spain's rule in Hispaniola divides into three separate periods. The first and by far the longest was from 1492 to 1795; at this last date the Spanish monarch ceded the eastern two thirds of the island to the French who had already been colonizing the western third (Saint-Domingue, Haiti) for a century. The second period, from 1810 to 1821, provided an uneasy interlude between the two occupations of the whole island by the revolted slaves of the French colony, the Haitians. The third and shortest period, from 1861 to 1865, represented an ill-advised attempt on the part of the Dominican government itself to be rid of the constant annexationist threats from Haiti and the major colonial powers by yielding voluntarily to the "Mother Country." Dominican historians refer to the second period as the reign of "España boba" (Foolish Spain), but the term could as well be applied to all three, and most aptly to the first, when Spain's rule was virtually unopposed and the colonial administrators did everything conceivable to hasten the rich island's disintegration.

The "events" of this long, remarkably eventless period are soon told. But what it was like to govern and be governed, to live or simply to exist in the limbo that Spanish Hispaniola had become during these centuries, has more of a bearing on the luridly eventful history that was to follow.

The powers of the governors who succeeded Diego Columbus were curtailed by the jurisdiction of a superior court, authorized to hear appeals even from the decisions of the governor himself. This *Audiencia,* as it was called, was originally established by King Ferdinand to block the possibility that the Columbus family might attempt to rule independently of the Crown. The powers of this council—over all matters political, civil, military, and criminal—were as absolute as those of any tribunal in the world; and along with the dreaded Inquisition, it shared ultimate power in the religious field as well. In 1509 the *Audiencia*'s jurisdiction extended over the whole Antilles and the adjacent coasts of the mainland; but in 1526, to curb the immense powers of Cortés, Mexico was given its own *Audiencia;* and later on rule over Central and South America was also excluded.

Between Diego Columbus' departure in 1524 and the first invasion by the Haitians in 1801 there were no less than fifty governors of Santo Domingo; but only one of them, Alonso de Fuenmayor, who later became archbishop, left anything to show for it. Between 1533 and 1556 this enterprising Spaniard completed the building of the cathedral and erected the walls and forts around the capital, some of which are still to be seen. He also repelled the pirates then beginning to infest the Caribbean and prey on its coastal cities. But within a quarter century of Fuenmayor's departure two disasters, one natural and one man-made, had undone most of his good works.

In 1564 the principal inland cities, Santiago de los Caballeros and Concepción de la Vega, were destroyed by earthquake. In 1586 Sir Francis Drake, commanding eighteen ships, landed near the mouth of Rio Haina, laid siege to the capital, sacked and looted it for a month, and when a ransom of 25,000 ducats ($30,000) for its return was delayed, systematically burned and tore down one third of the buildings. When Drake left with the ransom money, he took with him the city's bronze cannon and everything of value he could find in the churches. For good measure, he also hanged several friars.

The capital had to fight for its life once more in 1655, this time against a fleet sent out by Oliver Cromwell with instructions to make a permanent occupation. An army of nine thousand men was aboard the squadron ably commanded by Admiral William Penn, father of Pennsylvania's more pacific founder. Fortunately for the colonists, the two generals sent ashore, Venables and Buller, botched the envelopment, and after sustaining heavy losses, the English re-embarked and sailed for Jamaica, which they proceeded to take and turn into a British colony. Since 1630 sporadic raids by the French freebooters who were beginning to base themselves on Tortuga Island and the adjacent northwest coast of Hispaniola, had kept the colonists busy. During this period the Spanish rulers were so intent on monopolizing what was left of Hispaniola's commerce that they actually burned Puerto Plata, Monte Cristi, Fort Liberté, and Cap Haïtien to the ground merely to prevent smuggling!

Encouraged by the desert thus created along the north coast, the French buccaneers moved in. These nomads of the sea first took over the offshore island of Tortuga. Tortuga's settlements were several times destroyed by the Spanish, but by 1664, under the able D'Ogeron working for the French West India Company, and with the aid of the British in Jamaica, the colony on the western end of the main island was stabilized. Women from the Paris slums were brought over as wives for the colonists. Soon the French government was establishing courts and churches. By 1674 D'Ogeron had not only sent a punitive expedition into the Spanish colony, which captured and briefly held Puerto Plata and Santiago, but he was proposing to France that he be empowered to take over the whole island and make it a French colony. The Spanish colonists, who were to welcome the French as their saviors a little more than a century later, would probably have welcomed them now; they would certainly (as events were to prove) have been better off economically under French rule. But at this juncture D'Ogeron died, and the two mother countries made peace—temporarily.

Between 1685 and 1697 the war was on again. The French took Santiago and burned it to the ground for the second time. The Spaniards for their part marched west twice. Once, with the help of the English, they sacked Cap Haïtien and Port-de-Paix, the English carrying off all the men, the Spaniards the women and children. But in 1697, under the Treaty of Ryswick, Spain finally ceded the western end of the island to France, and in the hundred years that followed, the French were to organize their mountainous third of the island into the world's richest colony.

How is one to account for the fact that in this same century the largest, most favored part of the rich island reached its lowest depths? (By 1730 the population had dropped to an incredible six thousand.) For one thing, the nineteen thousand square miles had been parceled out to absentee landlords who did nothing with their huge "plantations" except permit the casual roundup of wild cattle for smuggling to the industrious French. For another, the sugar plantations along the south coast had been abandoned, partly because of the sacking of the ports by pirates; nor were any roads built which might have permitted the exploitation of the fertile Cibao. For still another, Spain's concentration of its civil, military, and religious establishment in the capital tended to attract enterprising men from the provinces —to serve and then to seek adventure and fortune abroad rather than suffer the hazards and boredom of agriculture. More important still, trade restrictions imposed by Spain had made export, except in the form of contraband, a losing proposition.

In 1740, with the opening of several ports to foreign commerce, things began to improve a little. A severe earthquake in 1751 destroyed the towns of Azua and Seibo and damaged the capital, but repair was rapid. Ratification of a permanent treaty with the French, and marking of the disputed boundary with permanent pyramidal stone markers, was another factor leading to economic recovery. By

1785 the population had increased to almost 150,000; 40,000 of these belonged to the ruling caste and about the same number were slaves.

The fact that free men outnumbered slaves by more than two to one in the Spanish part of the island, whereas in French Saint-Domingue five hundred thousand slaves, most of them fresh from the African jungles, were in an eight to one majority, had two consequences. On the one hand, French slaves could and did produce unparalleled agricultural wealth; there was no country on earth that could compete with French Saint-Domingue in the export of sugar, coffee, cacao, and dyestuffs. On the other, Spanish Hispaniola, living under no threat of a nightmarish insurrection, was able to develop without undue fear or repression. Most of the Spanish slaves, born and bred in Hispaniola, knew no other state of affairs than a relatively mild servitude. Under Spanish law a slave could easily buy his freedom. The freedmen, already in a majority, were of course Negroes or mulattoes. True, there was little social intercourse between the freedman, who was addressed as Señor, and the white resident or official who must be addressed as Señor Don (the poor white was a mere Don). But the harshly discriminatory racial laws of the French colony, by which the free mulattoes were kept in a constant state of humiliation and resentment, were unknown. Haiti today, after a century and a half of independence, is race bound and race conscious. The Dominican Republic is and has been throughout its history almost uniquely without prejudice.

In the final decade of the eighteenth century a French savant, who had already spent several years studying and writing a book about the social organism of Saint-Domingue, visited the Spanish colony. In the companion volume, although the Frenchman was far from complimentary to the Spanish ruling caste whose laws, religion, and habits he detested, he grudgingly admitted the Spanish superiority in the crucial matter of race relationships. "That prejudice with respect to colour," he wrote, "so powerful with other nations, among whom it

fixes a bar between the whites, and the freed people, and their de-
scendents, is almost unknown in the Spanish part of Santo-Domingo."
A master, as an act of religious piety, would often free some or all
of his slaves in his will. Mulattoes, but not Negroes as yet, were
admitted into the priesthood. Female slaves could be free on payment
of $250—an additional $12.50 covering children unborn if the slave
happened to be the mistress of her master. All slaves, it was observed, were treated "with a mildness unknown in the colonies of
other nations," partly because the master, realizing that the slave
could soon be as free as himself, "forebore to treat him with
superiority or undue harshness."

Mederic Louis Élie Moreau de St.-Mery, the French nobleman who
made these and other observations during the decade he spent in
Hispaniola, published his findings in Philadelphia, whither he had
fled following the slave insurrection in Saint-Domingue, between
1796 and 1798. The volume on the Spanish part of the island appeared first, and in English, prefaced by a list of patron-subscribers
that included John Adams, then vice president of the United States.
It has never been reissued. In both studies the author reveals himself
to be a remarkably acute and "modern" sociologist. He investigates
the archives (such as they were), reads the available histories and
documents, travels on foot and by horse to every part of both colonies,
weighs his findings—topographic, geologic, economic—against the
latest scientific theories, talks to the people as well as their rulers, and
cuts through a mass of superstition and folklore to a hard-headed
assessment of the backwardness afflicting rulers and ruled. Spaniards
if they bothered to read him—Moreau is scathing on the subject of
their disrespect for books—must have found him hopelessly preju-
diced in favor of France, for he concludes with a summary of arguments to make a Spanish-speaking colonist look with favor on French
annexation.* And Catholics must have been equally repelled by the

---

* "The state of the French colony sufficiently proves the value of this writer's
dreams, and I have not the least reluctance to declare, that, with the same means, and
equally clear of obstacles, the Spaniards of Santo-Domingo would yield in nothing to
the French who inhabit the same land. . . . My reproaches apply much less to the

undisguised scorn with which this French Protestant viewed their unwillingness or inability to better the condition of their flock:

> Here, as in all the rest of the Spanish dominions, the priests are excessively jealous of their authority, and they never fail to find pretexts for declaring the cause of religion to be interested in everything that their temporal interests suggest as a means of manifesting their power.
>
> The Spaniards have hardly any but religious books, and are very fond of the images of saints. Were we to form a judgment of them from their behaviour in public, from the affected devotion with which they tell their beads, or stop to recite the Angelus, we should certainly conclude that they despised the things of this world, and that their thoughts were totally engrossed by those of the world to come; but this veil is not close enough to hide hypocrisy, and it can deceive those only who allow this sort of profanation to assume the name of virtue.

Moreau's description of the ruling caste is equally unkind. "Insensible to all the treasures which surround them," he says, "they pass their lives without wishing to better their lot." The country men wear commonly a shirt, a sleeved waistcoat, "a pair of ticking breeches," and go barefoot; those in the city sport long coats of silk— hopelessly out of style, he implies.

> The general character of these people is a heterogeneous mass of meanness and pride. Crawling, servile to the last degree when occasion requires it, they affect haughtiness the same moment. They borrow, for instance, under the pretext, sometimes absolutely absurd, that what they borrow is for a sick person, things that they are too proud to ask for, and that their idleness will never permit them to repay. They are timid with their superiors, and with their inferiors insolently disdainful. Superlatively malicious, they carry their revenge to the very grave, not knowing that it is laudable to be great and generous, even to an enemy.

The women fare hardly better under the Frenchman's fastidious eye. They wear, he says, a petticoat "commonly black; a sort of gown,

---

Spaniards of the colony than to the government, which has done nothing to raise them from their mediocrity, but has in a manner abandoned them." M. L. E. Moreau de St.-Mery, *A Topographical and Political Description of the Spanish Part of Santo-Domingo,* trans. William Cobbett (Philadelphia, 1796), I, 307.

and a shift which does not always descend below the waist. Their fine long hair is sometimes braided, and sometimes tied up with a ribbon coming round the forehead." Taste, Moreau adds snobbishly, plays no part in the decoration of their heads, even when they adorn them with wild flowers; and the cheap jewelry, "which they admire with a sort of coquetry," is imported (third-hand) from the capital of the French colony. Though "ignorant of the art of pleasing," the Creole women "are extremely amorous, and equally jealous; and it seems that in this respect we may apply to them all that I have else-where said of the French creoles"—a languorous, promiscuous, ma-licious lot. If Moreau's description of the feminine Creole was ac-curate, it was hardly to be wondered at that the Spanish men "not-withstanding their celebrity as lovers, care but little about pleasing the beloved object."

Sumner Welles in his *Naboth's Vineyard* describes life in the Spanish colony at this time as having "a flavor of romance not equalled, nor perhaps approached, in the other colonies of the new world," but he cites no evidence to prove his point. A tradition of luxury remained in the capital, he says, but the economic basis for the tradition had vanished. The houses on the narrow, winding streets, their windows grilled but unglazed, were hermetically sealed at night to keep out the "unhealthful" air. By day the life of the family re-volved about the patio. "In the living rooms the walls were white-washed, ungarnished by hangings or other decoration." Furniture, imported from Spain, was carved and gilded in rococo ornateness. Lavishly dressed officials contrasted offensively with the slaves in rags who waited upon them. An evening stroll in the central plaza and High Mass on Sundays "afforded practically the only opportuni-ties for social intercourse."

Moreau de St.-Mery mentions only two forms of recreation in eastern Hispaniola—sleeping and dancing.

> The Spaniards of Santo-Domingo, take after dinner a little nap, which they call a *sieste*. This favorite custom, among a people always indolent, con-verts the populous places of the island into a desert, during the hours the inhabitants are, in some sort, tired of their existence.

The sleepers lie, he adds mordantly, on horses' skins, sleeping in spite of the stings and bites of tormenting insects.

The cultured Frenchman might have been more tolerant of music-making in ancient Hispaniola had he foreseen the age of the merengue, the cha-cha, and the jukebox. As it was, he describes the singing of the island as melancholy and monotonous. "They dance, but like morris dancers, to the sound of a hoarse guitar which all the time complains most grievously of the awkwardness of the fingers that squeeze it; or else to the sound of a calabash only, on which they freely exercise their inharmonious hands." The Frenchman's somewhat puritan sensibilities were offended still more by the *fandinguette,* where the performing ballerina would catch the hats of the spectators and pile them on her head until tipped for their return.

Moreau was on firmer ground ridiculing the "cures" for prevailing diseases. Smallpox, since the colonists refused to "make use of innoculation," was found to be widespread. It was treated by "rubbing the pox with hog's lard to hasten their maturity" and then "washing them with urine." As for syphilis, "the Spanish creoles make it a subject of pleasantry, and this is sufficient to prove that it is not rare among them." The cure for this terrible disease was less drastic— salad greens.

A typical Santo Domingo meal in the 1780-90's might consist of smoked pig or dried corned beef sprinkled with lime juice and boiled with pimentos; cassava, plantain, or Indian cornmeal in lieu of bread; no salad—the custom of *eating* salads was likened to the grazing of brutes. Chocolate, or raw rum (*taffia*) smuggled out of Saint-Domingue, provided the liquid refreshment. A jug of cane syrup generally replaced refined sugar on the table. The use of tobacco, both for smoking and chewing, Moreau found to be "unpleasantly" widespread, chewing causing the teeth, "otherwise so justly boasted of as one of the ornaments of beauty," to turn black.

The shortage of sugar may be understood when it is observed that Moreau found only twenty-two small mills in operation in the colony, employing a total of but six hundred slaves. Most of these "manufactories" produced only syrup. There was no exporting at all. Coffee, though bushes bearing a pound weight of berries were common, was imported from across the French border. Cotton, cacao, and tobacco were produced almost entirely for domestic consumption. But beef, from the vast *hattes* (Spanish *hatos*) in the interior, provided the whole French colony with sustenance and was at that time the sole commercial export of Spanish Hispaniola.

A word to describe the pattern that emerges from even a cursory view of life on these self-contained *latifundia* is "authoritarian." Aside from having to pay the king's tax (tithe), amounting to a one-tenth share of all crops, manufactures, and rents—and out of which the civil, military, and religious establishments were financed —the head of each plantation "was virtually a dictator, responsible only to himself." There was no practical way to enforce legislation governing the relation of the planters to each other or to the colonial government, much less the decrees designed to insure "fair" treatment of slaves. The practice of substituting bribery for taxation, since the tax collector had no real stake in the country, was already becoming widespread. The absence of roads made access to most plantations impractical. Visits to the capital might be undertaken annually; to Spain once in a lifetime. Newspapers did not exist. Private couriers carried what mail there was. Such education as existed took place in the family, unless the planter could afford to send his sons to Spain. The University of Santo Domingo offered, then as now, an occasional and casual curriculum. A planter supervised his overseers, whose business it was to see that the slaves or free laborers produced as much as possible. Protection against rebellious labor or raids from neighboring *hatos* depended upon the size of the small private army each individual planter was able to maintain and his ability to equip it with arms. The system "worked" so long as Spain was content to concern herself only with the residence of the governor-general and the *Real Audiencia,* the seat of the archbishop, and the headquarters of the twelve companies of Spanish veterans in the capital, letting the rest of the colony shift for itself. The establishment of a pattern—in which a future independent government, seeking to mobilize the resources of the country as a whole either by force or by consent, would find it impossible to govern—was already set.

Commenting on the disparity between the little French colony with its 600,000 inhabitants and 250,000,000 *livres* of foreign trade, and the big Spanish one barely able to sustain a population of 125,000, Moreau came to two conclusions. The first was indisputable. If, as a reading of Las Casas had informed him, the primitive island with no organized agriculture at all, had been able to provide for its three million Indians, or even a third that number, it was clear "that the Spanish part, which makes up more than three-fifths of the island, should contain about 700,000 souls, more than six times its present population." Fourteen thousand Negro slaves were obviously inadequate. "A million and a half at the very least would be wanted to bring the Spanish part to a perfection proportioned to that of the French part!" But alas, the young intellectual lamented,

> Spain, of all the powers possessing colonies, has the weakest means of procuring negroes, since she has neither settlement nor factory on the African coast, and is reduced to receive all she does receive at second hand, she who first fell on the means of making negroes cultivate the lands of America.

Could he have foreseen the holocaust that was to come from French Saint-Domingue's "advantage," and the racial harmony that Santo Domingo enjoys to this day from its inability to capitalize on the slave trade, Moreau de St.-Mery might have been less sure which colony was destined to inherit the future.

III

Black Hispaniola, 1786-1822

The Haitian Invasions to the Occupation under Boyer

The chain of events that overwhelmed the island between 1789, when the French Revolution broke out, and 1844 when the Dominican Republic was born, had repercussions far beyond Hispaniola. Not only was the history of the three great colonial powers—Spain, France, and England—as well as of the newly formed United States, deeply affected. There was also set in motion that fundamental conflict between the white and colored races which continues, unresolved, into our time. Since the Spanish part of the island during this period was acted upon rather than acting, our focus in the present chapter necessarily shifts to the French part.

In 1789 both parts of the island were enjoying prosperity. The underpopulated Spanish part was, as we have seen, not only on the verge of an economic revival but close to drifting out of the institution of slavery without racial rancor. Unfortunately for the colonists, both trends were to be nullified by the tidal wave of revolution from abroad—a cataclysm that also engulfed the first faint stirrings of liberal enlightenment in Spain itself.

By 1789 the French colony of Saint-Domingue was supplying two thirds of the imports and exports of France, a volume of foreign trade greater than that of the newly freed thirteen American colonies combined. Seven hundred ocean going vessels were carrying across the Atlantic most of the sugar, coffee, cotton, and indigo consumed in Europe. The ostentatious wealth of the thirty-six thousand white landlords in the colony not only excited the envy of the rival colonial powers; it was becoming a source of growing irritation to the Court of Versailles itself. A century before, Louis XIV had attempted to ameliorate the condition of the Negro slaves in the French colonies by specifying that freedmen should enjoy every right of French citizenship. There were close to thirty thousand such freedmen in Saint-Domingue by 1789, and they owned between a fourth and a third of the property in the colony. The Code Noire, however, had been interpreted locally in such a way that the freedmen, most of whom were mulattoes, were being treated as social pariahs. Not only were they "segregated" in the schools, churches, and courts; they were barred from purchasing munitions or carrying sidearms—the privilege of a "gentleman." Louis XV acquiesced in these discriminatory racial laws, even making it difficult for the wealthy mulatto planters to travel and educate their children in France. Caught between their bitter resentment of the whites and their fear of the five hundred thousand statusless Negro slaves (many of whom they now owned and treated with at least as much cruelty as the whites did), the mulattoes were ready to take advantage of any opportunity to achieve their disregarded rights.

It was no wonder that all three castes in the colony saw their opportunity in the outbreak of the revolution in France. The white planters, chafing under increasingly onerous trade tariffs, hoped for self-government. The *affranchis* (freedmen) took the idealistic Declaration of the Rights of Man to mean that their abrogated privileges as French citizens would be immediately recognized. The slaves, as tension between the two castes of their oppressors progressed toward violence, bided their time.

They had not long to wait. The *grands blancs* made an initial blunder. Nominating no less than thirty-seven deputies to the states-general and demanding autonomy for themselves, they succeeded in alienating the moderate revolutionaries in Paris. The radical "desegregationists" there, banded together in a society called "The Friends of the Blacks," forced through a resolution guaranteeing the *affranchis* their long-withheld rights. Just as the white colonists were on the point of declaring their outright independence of France, two mulatto leaders, Ogé and Chavannes, encouraged during a visit to France by the radical Jacobins, organized a public demonstration in Saint-Domingue's capital. In March of 1791 the two mulattoes were seized and publicly broken on the wheel. Tension now spread from Cap Français (Cap Haïtien) throughout the colony. In May came the news that the National Assembly in Paris had decreed that mulattoes must be admitted to representation in the colonial assemblies. The governor-general of Saint-Domingue, under pressure from the infuriated white planters, suspended operation of the assemblies. The freedmen, with no alternative now but direct action, were preparing to organize a mulatto uprising when the Negro slaves themselves revolted.

Between that fateful August day in 1791 and January, 1793, when the guillotining of Louis XVI precipitated war by legitimist England and Spain against France, the situation in Hispaniola was as follows. In the northwest the terrified whites, their plantations burned, cowered behind a ring of forts in the capital city. In the southwest, for decades a stronghold of mulatto property owners, the cultured and talented military leader Rigaud was beginning to consolidate his local sovereignty. Rigaud neither abolished slavery nor cut himself off entirely from those leaders of the slave insurrection in the north who might have to be bargained with should the whites be expelled. In the remote Spanish colony eastward across the high mountains nothing seemed to have changed. Some of the wealthy planters, alarmed by reports of the murderous uprising, had taken the precaution of sending their families to Cuba. The governor was congratulating himself on his astuteness in welcoming those revolted Negroes who had been driven across the border by the French; he incorporated them into his modest garrison as auxiliaries and even gave some of their leaders commissions in the army of Spain.

But in 1793 two events occurred which made it forever impossible for the "old order" to re-establish itself in Hispaniola. In the grip of its own Reign of Terror, Jacobin France sent civil commissioners to the embattled colony. One of these, the fanatical abolitionist Sonthonax, took it upon himself to "free" the hordes of leaderless exslaves besieging Cap Français and let them into the city. Sonthonax issued his "Emancipation Proclamation" in violation of his instructions from Paris—not out of compassion for the maltreated blacks, but because the mulattoes and whites, who distrusted him, were about to engineer his deportation to France. The result was twofold. Many of the colonists, driven to the sea, were forced to emigrate, leaving control in the north to the French Army, now dependent upon a working agreement with the Negroes in the plain. The mulattoes, for their part, unwilling to share leadership with the chiefs of the more numerous blacks, withdrew to the south, thus insuring an eventual showdown along racial lines.

The other crucial event of 1793 was the outbreak of war in Europe. The English, hoping to prevent the spread of libertarianism to their own colonies, invaded Saint-Domingue, establishing beachheads at Môle St. Nicholas and Jérémie. With the help of runaway slaves in the surrounding high mountains, they captured Port-au-Prince. This had the effect of further isolating the mulatto south. The northern Negro leaders were meanwhile drawing closer to the French governor-general, Laveaux, in the common cause of repelling an invading power, one of whose aims appeared to be the reimposition of chattel slavery. Before they were to withdraw from Hispaniola five years later, these entirely futile operations of the British were to cost them forty-five thousand lives and $100,000,000.

The stage of history was now set for the brief, meteoric career of the first Negro of genius. Toussaint Louverture was a man so enigmatic in character that even today judgment as to whether he was hero or villain, devil or saint, depends upon the stance of the observer. Since Louverture's first appearance on the scene was in the Spanish colony, and since he crowned his career by conquering it and thus briefly uniting Hispaniola, a sketch of the little that is known of him will not be out of place.

François-Dominique Toussaint, already fifty years old when the events so far related were taking place, was born on a plantation near the capital of Saint-Domingue. He received the nickname "L'Ouverture" later, either in recognition of his capacity to "open" a way to freedom through the enemy's defenses or because of his missing front teeth. As stableboy and later coachman to a certain Bayou de Libertas, he appears to have been given the leisure to learn to read and write a little and was well treated, for in the early days of the insurrection (in which he took no part), he helped his master and mistress to escape and thereafter provided for them while they were in exile. Toward the close of 1791 he attached himself to the northern army of ex-slaves headed by Jean-François, and when that army was driven across the border, Toussaint enlisted with them in the Spanish auxiliary forces. Rising rapidly through the ranks, by 1794 he had under his command a black corps of four thousand men, the best trained and disciplined in the Spanish Army.

Short, ugly, puritanical, taciturn but witty, the Negro general had great natural dignity and courage and that unrivaled capacity to make quick, sound decisions without revealing his intentions that made him a leader of men, acknowledged as such by whites and blacks alike. Those who fell under Toussaint's spell, either on the battlefield or in political conclave, generally yielded to his persuasive powers. Singularly free from racial prejudice—he invited the white planters to return and manage their estates, he employed mulatto generals even when breaking the mulatto power in the south—he never wavered in his conviction that the island should be governed in behalf of its numerical majority, the Negro cultivators.

It is in the means used to achieve these ends that judgments of Toussaint's character still differ. Was he, as many claimed, a man of unscrupulous duplicity, using the black man's independence and the unity of the island merely as steppingstones to absolute power? Or was he, as Wordsworth's memorable sonnet declared, the immortal friend of "exultations, agonies, / And love, and man's unconquerable mind."

The enigma of Toussaint Louverture confronts us at the first moment of his life of which there is documentary record. Toussaint was a lifelong Catholic, and on May 2, 1794, the Spanish general, the Marquis d'Hermona, observing the fervor of his religious devotions, wrote: "In this whole world God has never entered a soul more pure." Just four days later Toussaint's brigade fell upon those Negro troops still loyal to Spain and routed them. Overrunning that part of northern Saint-Domingue still occupied by Spain, he joined forces with General Laveaux at Cap Français. Not only was the Spanish power in the island thus broken (a *fait accompli* that set the stage for Spain's formal relinquishment of its colony to France the following year), but the English, now faced with the overwhelming numbers of a nation-in-arms, began the disengagement that ended with their evacuation of Hispaniola in 1798. Did Toussaint "defect," fatally exposing his friends and protectors in exchange for Laveaux's promises of higher rank and a share in the island's rule? Or was it that the granting of full French citizenship to all Negroes in the colonies as a result of the ratification of emancipation by the national convention in Paris caused Toussaint to realize that between Jacobin France and the reactionary colonial policies of England and Spain there could be but one choice?

If the about-face of Toussaint caused consternation among the white colonists of Spanish Santo Domingo, it can be imagined what effect was made upon their deteriorating morale by the news of the Peace of Basel. It was as if an earthquake had been followed by a tidal wave, inundating the last safe positions, cutting off the remaining avenues of escape inland. There remained but one place to go —out. When the terms of the treaty by which Spain formally ceded its oldest colony in the New World to France were confirmed, those colonists with the wherewithal to do so precipitately embarked with all their transportable belongings for Cuba, Puerto Rico, or Venezuela. Sporadic insurrections among the few slaves still left in the Spanish colony were now taking place. In April of 1796 the French Commissioner Roume arrived in Santo Domingo to work out the details of turning over the colony formally to Laveaux and Toussaint.

Why had Spain given in so easily? As already indicated, there was not much to lose. Neglect and maladministration over 250 years had turned a tropical paradise into a desert—depopulated, debt ridden, without hope. The enlightened bureaucracy of Charles III, which had given promise in the 1780's of lifting the dense cloud of ignorance and sloth that had settled on Spain for two centuries, was suppressed by his successor, the imbecilic Charles IV. Spain's revival as a colonial and naval power depended on checking the growing ascendancy of Great Britain, and this could only be accomplished with the support of France. But Charles IV was so outraged by the threat to monarchy posed by the execution of Louis XVI, and so frightened by the libertarian fervor of the French Revolution, that he joined the first coalition against his neighbor. Not only did his disaffected troops fail to "liberate" the royalist provinces of southern France; the Jacobin armies crossed the Pyrenees and advanced almost to the Ebro. The resulting Treaty of Basel, through which the Queen's lover, the inept and profligate Godoy, capitulated to France, not only sealed the fate of Spain's colonial empire—Louisiana and Trinidad soon went the way of Santo Domingo—but opened the way for Nelson's annihilation of Spain's maritime power and Napoleon's eventual conquest of Spain itself.

Before Toussaint could move his troops eastward to take physical possession of the languishing eastern provinces, he had work to do at home. The English must be induced to leave their three bridgeheads. The mulatto south under Rigaud must be brought into line. And Laveaux—what to do about this friendly French republican who, as governor and military commander, was Toussaint's nominal chief?

He dealt with the English first. In a series of brilliant campaigns and even more brilliant diplomatic maneuvers, Toussaint succeeded in forcing their withdrawal. The new American nation, anxious to curtail both British and French power in the Caribbean, aided Toussaint generously with arms and trade arrangements. A quick campaign against Rigaud was entrusted to the lieutenant governor's ablest captain, the savage Dessalines. Dessalines, unlike Toussaint, Christophe, and most of the other leaders of the ex-slaves, had not been born in the Indies, but in the jungle of Africa, suffering all the horrors of the middle passage. He hated the cultured and arrogant mulattoes with only a little less uncompromising virulence than he reserved for the whites. In a campaign of unprecedented ferocity— women were raped and then butchered with their children, and such leaders as failed to escape by sea were mutilated or sawed between planks—Dessalines presented his chief with a "pacified" province. Toussaint had originally asked his mulatto general, Clairveaux, to undertake the assignment, but Clairveaux had refused. Enigmatic as ever, Toussaint entered Les Cayes on August 1, 1800, to the ringing of church bells, celebrated Mass, and remarked sadly that he had ordered Dessalines "to prune the tree, not to uproot it." His own policy, once he regained control, was humane and racially unbiased. But a great damage had been done. Those mulattoes who had escaped would soon be fighting against him. Their descendants for generations to come would reside (and rule) in Haiti as a race apart.

His treatment of Laveaux, however, was to have consequences more immediate and decisive in Toussaint's eventual downfall. In the subtle guise of bestowing honors upon his French colleague, Toussaint had him nominated representative of the colony to the French Assembly in Paris. No sooner was Laveaux gone than Toussaint assumed his powers—civil and military—for life. By so doing, the Negro dictator made it clear to Bonaparte, whose star was now on the ascendant in France, that Hispaniola would never provide the passkey to his dream of a revived French colonial empire in the West so long as this "gilded African," as Napoleon called him, merely paid lip service to French rule.

The way now seemed clear for Toussaint to incorporate Spanish Santo Domingo under his sovereignty. Bonaparte had expressly forbidden him to do so, but this was all the more reason why the Negro general felt obliged to protect his eastern flank. It was already clear that the First Consul might attempt to recapture France's richest overseas possession—if peace with England should give him the chance. The *Real Audiencia* had been transferred from Santo Domingo to Puerto Principe in Cuba in 1799; but the Spanish governor, General Joaquin García, remained in Santo Domingo, and, encouraged by the French commissioner, Roume, he gave every sign that he intended to remain there. After contriving Roume's arrest, Toussaint in January of 1801 crossed the border with two armies. The northern prong was commanded by his nephew, Moyse, the southern prong by himself. On January 27, Toussaint entered the capital and took possession, meeting with little resistance. The French tricolor was raised and a *Te Deum* was chanted in the cathedral. Toussaint then permitted Governor García to embark for Cuba with the remnants of the Spanish civil and military establishment.

Popular prejudice to the contrary, Toussaint's brief rule over the former Spanish colony was remarkably enlightened. The picture of him at the cathedral drawn for us by the notably race-prejudiced Sumner Welles—entering the gates "with simian self-importance," "his bloodshot eyes rolling with religious ecstasy," and "passing the members of the feminine sex in review"—is not borne out by the available evidence. Antonio Delmonte y Tejada, an eyewitness, describes Toussaint's blue uniform, flesh-colored cloak, and French Republican cockade. Then he adds:

Toussaint's graciousness and courtesy contributed much towards easing the situation. His bearing was martial, his aspect noble and imposing, his expression benevolent. His manner was friendly and unconstrained, yet dignified. When addressed by an officer of lower rank, he would incline towards him and listen affably. He graciously acknowledged the marks of respect shown to him, but seemed to wish to avoid special recognition.

Forty thousand inhabitants, more than a third of the total population, had already forsaken the colony. Toussaint made every effort to induce them back. He did his best to reassure the few planters who had remained. The return of prosperity to the French colony under Toussaint's rule had been astonishing. Under his policy of iron discipline for labor and a free hand (short of reintroducing slavery or wielding political power) to the returning emigrées, Saint-Domingue had in three years surpassed even its slave-state record of export trade. Toussaint hoped to awaken a similar spirit of industry in the long-sterile eastern provinces. Considering that the white planters in the Spanish part gave him little or no cooperation, he accomplished wonders. The mild mulatto Clairveaux and Toussaint's own brother Paul were appointed governors in Santiago and the capital. Their instructions during the invasion had been to avoid bloodshed; now they were told to exercise conciliation. Both orders were obeyed. "I have never considered," said Toussaint, liberating the Spanish slaves, "that liberty is synonymous with license." No doubt he was thinking of those leaderless Negroes who had become loafers or brigands after the first uprisings in the French colony. "Men who have gained their liberty," he added, do not have "the right to live in idleness and create disorder." He decreed that landowners must plant export crops immediately, and he organized a rural police to see that they did. On a tour of the Spanish territories he preached a gospel of work that had never been heard in the land before. Toussaint took personal responsibility for the security of life and property. He permitted those who wished to leave to take their moveable belongings with them. The people were given their own Appeals Court. Import and export duties were lowered drastically to 6 per cent, a figure well below that in the former French colony. For the first time in centuries contraband trade was eliminated by an efficient maritime patrol. Sugar cultivation in the French style was introduced. Roads that had become mere trails were repaired, and a fine new one connecting the capital with Dajabon was constructed. Carriages came into general use for the first time in the colony's history.

The abolition of custom lines alone would have been enough to have insured a measure of prosperity. And that came. But the land-owners continued to emigrate, not wishing to be ruled by men they considered their social and racial inferiors. Legend has it that Tous-saint, in despair of bringing the economic standards of the eastern part of the island up to those of the west, contemplated a general massacre of the recalcitrant whites, countermanding his decision only when a sudden thunderstorm alarmed his superstitious nature. But the legend is not in keeping with Toussaint's character. Fear, and the first faint stirrings of nationalism, were indeed factors in dis-turbing his rule—and insurance that if Bonaparte invaded, he would be assisted by a Spanish "Fifth Column."

Time was running out for Toussaint. The preliminaries to the Peace of Amiens, signed at London on October 1, 1801, freed the First Consul's hands. It was said at the time that if Bonaparte had sent Laveaux back to Saint-Domingue with a small force of three thousand men, he could have had what he needed. Toussaint, always reasonable and ready to bargain, would have given French capital limitless concessions. But it was not to be. The French dictator always thought first in terms of military advantage: surprise and envelopment. Toussaint, with many well-armed divisions, seemed to stand in the path of his ambition to conquer the North American continent. A combination of ruthlessly applied modern striking power and political treachery could do Toussaint in. And in the short run it did.

On January 29, 1802, Toussaint stood with his aides on a peak overlooking Samaná Bay to watch the arrival of the advance guard of the gigantic armada dispatched against him. What he saw—the number of vessels required to carry and supply twelve thousand of the picked veterans of the armies of the Rhine and of Italy—terrified him beyond belief. "We must perish," he cried to his staff, "all France is coming to San Domingo. She has been deceived; she comes to take vengeance and enslave the blacks!" The sagacious old warrior was right on the last count. Napoleon had included in his detailed orders to the commander, his brother-in-law, General Leclerc, instructions *not* to re-enslave the Negroes; but he had already decided otherwise, and this was the political error that would lead to the utter failure of the militarily flawless operation. Toussaint, for his part, was to be guilty of two fatal mistakes: On the very day that the great expeditionary force sailed from Brest, he had executed his nephew, General Moyse, for demanding a share in the land for the rank-and-file Negro and mulatto soldiers at the expense of the whites. By so doing, like Robespierre, he not only destroyed his own left wing, but he divided the loyalty of the commanders on whose allegiance in adversity he would soon have to depend. Psychologically tranquillized by his serene relationship with the republican Laveaux, Toussaint closed his eyes to the fundamental changes that had occurred in France during the Thermidorian reaction to Jacobinism. So instead of arming the Negro masses in preparation for effective guerilla warfare, he relied on his regulars, outclassed by the Napoleonic veterans and quick to accept seemingly generous peace terms. And when an "honorable" capitulation was finally offered to Toussaint himself, he accepted in good faith, only to be kidnaped and shipped off to die in jail in the French Alps.

The French conquest of the Spanish part of Hispaniola was entrusted by Leclerc to two officers—Kerverseau, who had once served under Toussaint, and Ferrand. Paul Louverture was tricked into surrendering the capital, and Clairveaux, apparently at the instigation of the bishop of Santo Domingo who had long been working on the weak mulatto general, surrendered without a fight. Had Saint-Domingue not then received the news that Napoleon had indeed reintroduced slavery to the other French colonies in the Caribbean and had every intention of doing the same in Hispaniola, it is conceivable that the French might have coped with the epidemic of yellow fever which was beginning to decimate their victorious army. As it was, disease—and the now aroused Negro population's resorting to effective action—was too much for them. General Rochambeau, Leclerc's successor in command, attempted a final campaign of extermination, even importing packs of man-eating bloodhounds from Jamaica to pursue the Negroes into the mountains; but it was too late. He was defeated in battle by Dessalines at Vertières on November 18, 1803, and Dessalines soon took his logical revenge by ordering the extermination of every white man, woman, and child remaining in Saint-Domingue.

For a while Spanish Santo Domingo held out against Dessalines. The idea of disobeying orders from Paris to return home and instead retaining the eastern provinces for France was conceived in the mind of Ferrand, the general left in charge in the Cibao. Hearing that in the capital Kerverseau was about to capitulate to Dessalines, Ferrand marched thither and placed his fellow general aboard ship for Puerto Rico. Ferrand was an enterprising soldier and an able administrator, but he was quick to reintroduce slavery, and even decreed that Negroes over fourteen crossing the old French border into the Spanish part should be enslaved. Dessalines invaded, won a quick battle at the Yaque del Sur River, and laid siege to Santo Domingo on March 5, 1805. Christophe, meanwhile, struck north through the Cibao, taking Santiago and massacring those landlords, local officials, and priests who had hopefully taken refuge in the church. At La Vega he was ordered to return home, which he did, burning everything in his path as he marched westward.

The capital was saved, and Dessalines retreated to the border, not so much because a French squadron under Admiral Missiessy fortuitously appeared in the harbor, as because he received word that an even larger French squadron was entering the harbor of Gonaïves and that Saint-Domingue—Haiti, as he now called it—was in danger of being re-enslaved.

It is just barely conceivable that Toussaint Louverture may some day come to be regarded by the Dominican people as one of their own heroes, but there is no chance at all that Dessalines will ever be so regarded. One might go a step further and say that until the modern Haitians themselves are prepared to make this distinction and elevate the neglected Toussaint to the pinnacle they now reserve exclusively for the bloodthirsty Congo racist, Dessalines, there will never be real understanding between the two countries. Toussaint's aims—racial equality, prosperity through efficient large-scale agriculture, resistance to foreign imperialisms—are the aims of Dominican liberals. Dessalines' program—black supremacy, military communism (two thirds of the population condemned to peasantry and forced to work for the remaining third, the dictator's army), and total isolation from Western civilization—had its foreseeable results. In 1805 Dessalines had himself crowned emperor (*"Moi seul, je suis noble!"*). In 1806 he was assassinated by the small hierarchy of educated mulattoes without whose literacy and technical aid even he had been unable to rule. The once-thriving estates were divided and subdivided among the cultivators to the point of economic no return. And the army of illiterate mercenaries was kept intact, a perpetual assurance that there would be neither democracy at home nor peace for Haiti's defenseless neighbor.

Now began the first of countless attempts on the part of foreign powers to fill the vacuum in eastern Hispaniola. Ferrand was determined to give the scanty populace something worth fighting for. He secured Napoleon's backing, but this proved to be a double liability. Not only were the coastal cities now subjected to constant blockade and attack by the British; it was inevitable that Dessalines' successors—Pétion and Christophe, who had divided Haiti between them—would do everything in their power to prevent stability in a potential base for reconquest.

Ferrand encouraged resettlement of the abandoned areas. He established schools. He even built waterworks for the capital—a project that would have to wait a century to be completed. He persuaded many of the *émigré* families to return, but this too backfired: most of them were Spanish royalists, sentimentally or through self-interest, and they at once engaged in conspiracies to oust the liberal French governor. In October of 1808 a Cotui planter, Juan Sánchez Ramírez, liberally supplied with munitions by both Pétion and Christophe, raised the Spanish flag over El Seybo. The Spanish in Puerto Rico helped. So did the English, seizing Samaná and raising the *Spanish* flag there and then applying a tight blockade to the capital lest the French attempt reinforcement. Ferrand marched out of the capital to confront the rebels in El Seybo, but on the way some of his native forces deserted. He was met at Palo Hincado on November 7 by Sánchez Ramírez and Pedro Santana the Elder, and defeated. He committed suicide. On July 9, 1809, the last French in the capital were overcome by the British and the country once more became a dependency of Spain.

The thirteen years of renewed neglect, misrule, and outright scavenging that now began were so devoid of ameliorating reform that even Hispanophiles were quick to concur in christening them *España boba*. Commenting on the paradoxes involved in the take over, Sumner Welles remarked:

> It is an astonishing fact that at the very moment when freedom from the control of Spain was being sought by many of the other Spanish colonies of the American Continent, when revolutions were breaking out in Buenos Aires, Venezuela, Nueva Granada, and Mexico, when the cry of "liberty and independence" was being eloquently proclaimed by Bolívar, and the death knell of the period of Spain's colonial expansion had already sounded, the colony of Santo Domingo, in freeing itself from France, should have demanded its return to the Government of Spain.

Ferrand's one reactionary policy, the reimposition of slavery, remained in full force; but the prosperity that had accompanied his otherwise enlightened rule vanished overnight. Cane, coffee, and cacao production came to a standstill. Poverty became so widespread that class distinctions almost ceased to exist. The only redeeming feature, if it was one, was that more of the exiled families returned to occupy their former estates.

For nine weeks in 1821 a conspiracy led by the lawyer José Núñez de Cáceres, with Haitian help, turned the colony into the state of Spanish Haiti, affiliated with the Republic of Colombia. The Spanish governor was arrested and shipped back to Spain. But Núñez de Cáceres, receiving no help at all from Colombia, was forced to turn for recognition to Pétion's successor in Haiti, the mulatto general Jean-Pierre Boyer. Boyer's answer was quick, simple, and from Haiti's point of view, logical. "The whole island," he said, "should constitute a single republic under the flag of Haiti." And to emphasize the point, Boyer at once sent armies from the north and south across the undefended border.

There was no resistance. Boyer had already guaranteed the slaves their freedom. The other colored people and the poor whites may have had mixed feelings, but they had no stomach for being subjected anew to the barbarities that had followed resistance to the armies of Christophe and Dessalines a generation before. The Spanish garrison had departed with the Spanish captain-general. On February 9, 1822, Núñez de Cáceres, with no other alternative, handed the keys to the city of Santo Domingo to the Haitian commandant—literally on a silver platter. The twenty-two years of spiritless, degrading, and anarchic occupation that were to culminate in the birth of a new nation, had begun.

IV

Liberation, 1822-44

Juan Pablo Duarte and the
First Failure of Liberalism

The Haitian occupation of the Spanish-speaking part of Hispaniola was doomed from the start. Language differences, the Haitian injection of the racial question, the abysmal failure of Boyer's *Code Rural,* all played a part.

The language barrier by itself need not have proved insuperable. The traditions and cultural associations surrounding the two languages had not, at best, penetrated deeper than the small ruling groups. By 1822 the ruling groups in both countries had been either destroyed or dispersed, and for a whole generation the government bureaucracy in Santo Domingo had been actually conducting its business in the language of the Haitians.

The racial question was another matter. For the predominantly black Haitians to rule amicably over a small neighbor already "mixed" in color, and having an educated minority almost entirely white, would have required unprecedented tact. Toussaint displayed tact; but there is no record of any other Haitian proconsul even being aware of the meaning of the word. Boyer's troops came to occupy and exploit a conquered province. His soldiers were not even paid;

their first preoccupation was to live off the land, and to live as comfortably as possible. There was nothing in the background of the typical black ex-slave to make him sympathize with the light-skinned vassal—on the contrary! By treating the Spanish-speaking upper class with indifference or contempt, the Haitian no doubt felt he was balancing accounts. The mulattoes among the occupying civil servants could scarcely be expected to act generously. What culture they possessed was French, and here was a people that had not only been ungrateful enough to rebel against its enlightened French friends, but had made a point of insisting that Spanish culture be regarded as sacred. The mulattoes, moreover, would have been more than human had they failed to take advantage of this opportunity to buy off the natural resentment of the illiterate black majority of Haitians in whose name they ruled. Give the black army in Santo Domingo a free hand (Boyer must have reasoned), and the supremacy of the colored elite in Port-au-Prince could survive unchallenged.

As for the *Code Rural,* it was an expression on the one hand of Boyer's determination to be a gentle ruler, eschewing the brutal compulsions of Christophe and Dessalines, and on the other of his quixotic hope to foster industry and prosperity through legislation alone. The Code was promulgated in 1826, after Haiti had teetered to the brink of economic ruin under seven years of *laissez faire.* It was designed to arrest the subdivision of the land that had been going on under Pétion. The basic provision of the Code was to attach each inhabitant—with the exception of the soldiers, the bureaucracy, and the landed "aristocracy"—to the soil, under contract to the proprietor of the land or the lessee thereof. Workers who malingered or failed to fulfill their quota could be jailed by the soldiers whose duty it was to enforce the provisions of the Code on each estate.

Similar serfdom under Toussaint and Christophe had "worked"— that is, it had brought prosperity. Under the easy-going Boyer, it failed. The explanation is simple: Boyer did not enforce the law. The workers ignored it. The small planters (most of the large estates had already been broken up) ignored it. The remaining large holders balked at surrendering to the state even so little as a fourth of the crop. The Spanish-speaking peoples, unfamiliar with forced labor, would have none of it. On top of this, Boyer signed an incredible treaty with France: in return for "recognition" (the promise not to reinvade), he not only turned over to France most of Haiti's cash reserves, he put his country into debt for the next sixty years. It was supposed that the army, thus freed from standing guard at the beaches, would now devote its energies to policing the Code. Instead, as a contemporary French historian put it, the soldiers

> . . . when they saw themselves freed, by a solemn treaty, from all attack on their coasts, seemed to allow their arms to drop relaxed at their sides, saying, *Let's take a rest.* The soldier who up to now had squeezed his body into a uniform and had subjected himself to European discipline, shouldering his arms, staring straight ahead as if seeing nothing, now began to leave unbuttoned the uniform which choked him, dragged a mattress into his sentry-box so that he might sleep through his watch, and let his cross slip to the earth never to pick it up again.

Those soldiers who took any action at all, robbed the cultivators blind, or took graft for not doing so. Back came small-scale farming and share cropping. Under French law, which lacked primogeniture, the plots became smaller and smaller. Government lands were abandoned. Cultivation of sugar, coffee, and cotton became almost impossible. Gradually each peasant became his own master—master of the land poverty that condemned him to eternal peasanthood. By 1842 a French observer was thus able to describe the state of the island:

> The fields of Haiti are dead. There where under slavery thousands of tons of sugar were made, now one sees only a few crops and a little syrup to turn into raw rum. Lively growths of cactus cover with thorns the acres of cane, of fields, of pastures deserted by the hand of man; the cactus invades the towns, coming even up to the heart of the cities, flourishing in the midst of ruins, as if to insult the inhabitants. . . . On the one hand, no one cultivates with regularity, because everyone is discouraged by the thefts of cane and fruit by people without any moral discipline, and in a country without police; while on the other hand,

people complain of being poor, and of not being able to devote enough money to indispensable improvements. . . . And if the proprietors cannot even make work progress, imagine the condition of the poor!

Worse still, as the civil bureaucracy fell, perforce, into the hands of the educated mulattoes, the army, to balance off black resentment, became the exclusive property of the primitive peasant. Small wonder that Spanish Hispaniola became the scapegoat of the first and the plaything of the second.

There are few records of what life was like in the eastern part of the island under Boyer's occupation, but none of them paint a pretty picture. One, a report to Parliament in 1826 by the British Consul-General in Haiti, mentions the lack of civilian authority, the arrogance of the military, and the tyranny of the Code, adding:

> The decrease in population in thirty-three years has been very nearly one-third of the whole population in 1783. . . . The Government has appropriated all the church property to its own use. The clergy rely wholly on the fees, two-thirds of which they are obliged to pay into the Treasury. . . . It is not a subject of surprise that morality should be in as low a stage. . . . Marriage is scarcely thought of. . . .

Latin America, following the lead of Colombia, which had been snubbed by Haiti in the wake of the Núñez de Cáceres fiasco, broke off all relations with the occupied provinces. North American interest was confined to the activity of the abolitionist societies, which sent boatloads of ex-slaves to the depopulated country. Many of these died of typhus, but some settled in Samaná Peninsula where their English-speaking descendants remain to this day. This, combined with the normal sexual activity of the conquerors, appreciably darkened the complexion of the existing inhabitants. But the Haitian effort to build a strong African state in the whole island was progressing in this respect only; representation in the Haitian Congress, which was open to all, would no doubt have been declined by educated Spanish-speaking people, even if they could have been elected. As in the days before *España boba,* those planters who could afford to, emigrated. Those unable to leave themselves sent their children out of the country to be educated.

Among the latter was a young man soon destined to play the noblest, if not the most effective, role in his country's history. Born in 1813, and seventeen years of age at the time he took ship for New York and then Europe, Juan Pablo Duarte seems to have accepted the stifling atmosphere of Santo Domingo as normal. It was the trip abroad that opened his eyes, testifying at the outset to the essential romanticism and otherworldliness of his nature. To understand what awakened the ardent patriotism in Duarte, it is necessary to take account of the revolution then sweeping France. Not the political revolution—for the transition from the legitimist, clerical Charles X to the *petit bourgeois* constitutionalist Louis Philippe changed nothing—but the revolution of romanticism.

The literary gods of Paris in 1830 were Lamartine and the aging Chateaubriand. The rising star was Victor Hugo, then twenty-eight. Lamartine was a gifted poet; he was also a sentimentalist, a man who cultivated elevated sentiments not because they were true, but because they were beautiful. Chateaubriand was a royalist who had escaped the French Revolution to wander in the forests of the Mississippi making a cult of the Noble Savage. He returned home to become the darling of Napoleon, catering to his scheme of fostering political security by reviving Christianity. "Christianity," he wrote, "is the most poetical of all religions, the most fertile in literary, artistic and social results." Victor Hugo, educated in Spain, grew up a royalist and a Catholic, and though he was now preparing to enter into a calculated phase of conservative republicanism, he was to be the leader in that posthumous glorification of Napoleon which culminated in the return of the emperor's ashes to the Invalides in 1840. The riots occasioned by the first performance of Hugo's bombastic play *Hernani* on February 25, 1830, was the big event of the year. Although Duarte may not actually have attended the play, he must have been aware of this glorification of Spain's Emperor Charles V.

And he no doubt took cognizance of the coincidental fact that the first character to be revealed upon the stage is named—Duarte.

The literary character of the typical romantic hero was now well established. He must be a stranger among men, but an enemy of tyrants—from abroad. In politics and religion he must stand for legitimacy and ritual. But like the poet Heine, the typical romantic hero could also say: "Lay on my coffin a sword, for I was a brave soldier in the war of humanity." In token of his superiority to other men, he was invariably withdrawn, melancholy, and supersensitive.

Every one of these characteristics fits Duarte. Returning home in 1833 after a visit to Catalonia in Spain, where the statutes and liberties of that dissident province impressed him, Duarte announced to his startled friends that Santo Domingo would soon be as free and as liberally governed as any state on earth. Chief among these early friends was Juan Isidro Pérez, mentally unstable but passionately idealistic, who then and there decided to devote his life to Duarte and his cause.

The very qualities which were to completely disqualify Duarte from exercising power made him perfectly suited to the task of arousing his countrymen from their subservience to the slothful invaders. His intellectualism, his high seriousness and disdain for any of the frivolities or sensual pleasures of life, his preoccupation with philosophy, his naïve belief that "politics . . . is a *pure* and noble science," his pietism—all removed Duarte beyond the pale of Haitian suspicions; while his unshakable integrity and obvious lack of selfish motives, his mysticism, and his predeliction for Masonic numerology made him the ideal instigator of a secret conspiracy.

As late as 1838 the Haitians ignored the revolutionary movement in their midst. The "Trinitaria," a secret society organized in self-contained groups of three, with passwords, codes, and a declaration signed in blood, conducted public demonstrations in the guise of religious observances. A flag was devised with white, the color torn out of the French emblem by Dessalines, imposed upon the red and green quarterings as a cross, symbolizing the purity of Christ's ideals. When the "Trinitaria" was denounced to the Haitian commandant by the traitor Felipe Alfáu, its place was quickly taken by a new society, "La Filantrópica," which carried on libertarian propaganda even more effectively by producing plays filled with subversive soliloquies and *double-entendres*. In 1841, "Dominicans" residing in Venezuela gave financial help.

In May of 1842 a fearful earthquake destroyed Santiago in the east and Cap Haïtien in the west. The resulting panic in both parts of the island provided an ideal accompaniment for the emergence of underground opposition. Duarte contacted the anti-Boyer faction of Haitians in Les Cayes. This move, had it succeeded in combining effectively the liberal elements in both countries, might have had incalculably benign effects in the century to follow, but it failed. Boyer was overthrown, but his successor, Rivière-Hérard, immediately made plans to hold in check the tide of disaffection in the east. Duarte, already in hiding in Santo Domingo, decided to leave the country for the time being. In Caracas, he tried to get help from the Venezuelans and Colombians, but was unsuccessful.

Leaving Caracas on December 15, Duarte sailed north as far as Curaçao, where he received news that his father, a well-to-do Spanish-born merchant, had died. Duarte's mother, who shared her son's idealism, now agreed to devote what was left of their family fortune to arms. Francisco del Rosario Sánchez and others of the separatists urged Duarte by letter to come to the port of Guayacanes at once. But at this critical moment Duarte, depressed and exhausted, suffered a violent cerebral fever that laid him low in the Dutch colony for weeks. In the light of subsequent events one might be inclined to diagnose this nervous breakdown in two ways. The unsympathetic could regard it as proof that Duarte's personality was incapable of facing reality, much less exercising power. His partisans would be quite as justified in interpreting it as a manifestation of that visionary insight of the true saint which balks at compromising with anticipated evil.

On the night of February 27, 1844, the conspirators, fearing to postpone their move lest it be betrayed to the Haitians, struck. The gate of "El Conde" was seized and its guard surrendered to Sánchez. Governor Desgrotte, surprised, evacuated the Ozama fortress and the city itself with little bloodshed. A few days later Azua, Santiago, and the other provincial cities capitulated. A central governing junta, presided over by the "Trinitario" Rámon Mella, was formed. On March 14 Duarte arrived in the port of the Ozama and on the following day entered the capital in triumph.

It was Duarte's first and last triumph. Collaborators with the Haitians, self-seekers who desired the support of one or another of the great powers, now came to the fore. For a time the junta was actually presided over by a former aide to Boyer. Buenaventura Baez and Pedro Santana, who were to succeed each other in power in the decades of misrule and betrayal to come, were already aspiring to office. Baez, in Azua, wanted a protectorate under France. Santana, along with Duarte, was given command of the army that was being quickly assembled to face the main Haitian concentration west of Azua. Although Duarte had made a romantic excursion into the tactics of the Napoleonic era while in France, he was an amateur soldier. He mistrusted Santana's hankering for foreign support, and he disagreed with Santana's feeling that only a defensive campaign could succeed in containing the vastly more numerical Haitians. Santana's brigade had already won a great but indecisive victory. Duarte and his own troops were eager to follow this up, to pursue the retreating Haitians to the border, but Duarte himself was unwilling to disobey the junta's orders. While he hesitated, Santana had his way, and the politicians, believing that Duarte was too "unrealistic" to command, recalled him.

With Sánchez in the presidency of the junta and officially replacing Santana as commander of the army of the south, Duarte was made governor of the Cibao, where General José María Imbert had already succeeded in repelling the northern army of Haitians under General Pierrot. But now again Duarte's incorruptible character made it impossible for him to take advantage of a threatening division of the new country. At Santiago a great crowd, including delegates from Puerto Plata, hailed him, and with Ramón Mella at its head begged him to assume the presidency in defiance of the temporizing elements in the capital. Duarte agreed, but only on condition that "a free election, by majority vote, and without pressure, shall elect me to this high office." This was on July 11. As he stood there in the hot dusty square, erect, proud, but deeply touched by the faith of these simple people, he delivered his last testimonial:

> Be happy, citizens of Puerto Plata, and my heart will be fully satisfied even without the office which you desire I may obtain; but first of all, be just, if you desire to be happy, for that is man's first duty; be united, and thus you will put out the flame of discord and conquer your enemies, and the fatherland will be free and safe, and your wishes will be gratified; so shall I obtain my greatest recompense, the only one to which I aspire: that of seeing you peaceful, happy, independent and free.

On July 12 Santana, refusing to relinquish his southern command to Sánchez, marched on the capital and had himself proclaimed dictator. Mella, hoping like Duarte to avoid a civil war, worked out a compromise by which Duarte and Santana would stand for election on the same ticket, as president and vice president respectively. But no sooner was the compromise agreed to than Santana threw Mella into prison and deprived Sánchez of the presidency of the junta. Duarte was arrested in Puerto Plata and dispatched to join the others in the *Torre del Homenaje* as a common criminal. Threatened with the death penalty should they ever set foot on Dominican soil again, Sánchez and Mella were exiled to England, Duarte placed aboard a vessel bound for Germany.

Nothing in the "liberated" country was now fundamentally different. Only the names and the complexions of the oppressors had changed.

The story of Juan Pablo Duarte during the thirty-two years of his life that were to follow is entirely in keeping with his incarnation as a lay saint and as the keeper of his country's conscience. One might go further and say that as Duarte's hitherto neglected story comes to be known, his pure, exemplary nature, rarer than those encompassing the martial ardors of Bolívar, San Martín and Martí, may become the spiritual inspiration of a regenerated Latin America.

An affecting scene took place at the Santo Domingo waterfront as Duarte was preparing to take ship. Juan Isidro Pérez, whose rage for liberty was already verging upon madness, threatened to commit suicide unless taken to his friend and hero. Throwing himself into Duarte's arms, he cried: "I know you are going to die, and obeying my reason I have come to die with you." In Hamburg, Duarte went to a home for poor sailors, along with Pérez and his other companions. But after another bout of nervous fever, during which he was cared for in the local masonic lodge, Duarte decided to return to the Caribbean alone. At his first port of call, St. Thomas in the Virgin Islands, he seems to have made the ultimate decision of renunciation. Exiles from Santana's tyranny tried to enlist his support, but he neither shared their passion for vengeance nor their belief that a civil war would result in more than bloodshed and mass misery. Resolving to commune with his troubled soul as far from the temptations of temporal compromise as possible, he took ship for Venezuela and traveled to a remote village on the Rio Negro, a tributary of the Amazon in the northern borderland of Brazil, where he was to live in complete obscurity for the next fifteen years.

Among the primitive people of the village where he now took up residence, Duarte seems to have found peace at last. Every one of his friends, after their fashion, had let him down; women, other than those of his family, played no part in the great ascetic's life. Duarte did penance for his youthful dreams of personal glory and national power among the unambitious savages and their children. Conducting classes for the latter, he made enough of a living to keep body and soul together, but only the soul grew strong. His friendship with a Portuguese missionary, San Gervi, strengthened the religious aspect of his mysticism.

Gervi's death in 1861 perhaps freed Duarte to undertake a final *rapprochement* with the world of men and his beleaguered country. He had already come back to Caracas in 1860. Four years later, hearing that Santana's reannexation of the Dominican Republic to Spain had been repudiated by a popular rebellion in the Cibao, Duarte took ship for Monte Cristi. Ascending the Yaque del Norte to Guayubín, he was received by General Benito Monción and taken to see Ramón Mella. Mella's enfeebled condition, in the setting of a wrecked, impoverished countryside, so shocked Duarte that he suffered another attack of the old fever. Recovering, he addressed a letter to Ulises Espaillat, liberal member of the provisional government in Santiago:

> Exiled from my native land by that band of paricides who, beginning by exiling the founders of the Republic, have concluded by selling to the stranger the country whose independence they swore to defend against all enemies, I have led during twenty years the nomad life of an exile, without previously obtaining from Providence the realization of the hope I have always fostered in my heart to be able to return one day to my fellow-citizens, to consecrate to the defense of their liberties what still remained of my strength and life. But there came the hour when Judas Iscariot believed that his work had been consecrated through his treason, and there came then for me the hour of my return to my country. God has made smooth my path notwithstanding the many difficulties and risks attendant upon my return. Here I am with four companions in this heroic town of Guayubín, ready to share with you in any way God may see fit all the vicissitudes and struggles which God may yet have in store, in the great task of restoring the independence of the Republic which you have already initiated with such honor and glory.

Taking horse for Santiago, Duarte now confronted the other members of the provisional government, already fighting among themselves over division of the spoils. None of them, with the exception of Espaillat, wanted to give the popular hero any share of the proceedings. In fact, it was all that Espaillat could do to get them to appoint the father of his country to a diplomatic post as Minister Plenipotentiary to the South American states. A libelous article in a Cuban monarchist newspaper, no doubt planted by those fearful of

Duarte's moral prestige at home, charged him with divisive intentions; the provisional government leaped at the opportunity of removing him once more from Dominican soil. But before setting sail for Caracas, by way of Haiti and Curaçao, Duarte addressed a farewell letter to his countrymen:

> If I returned to my country after so many years of absence, it was solely for the purpose of serving her with my soul, my life, and my heart, preaching as I always have, love among all the Dominicans. It was never my purpose to be a cause of discord nor a motive for dissension.

Duarte had not even arrived in Caracas when it began to be clear to him that his post carried little authority. A second Minister Plenipotentiary, Melitón Valverde, crossed paths with him at Curaçao, and while Duarte tarried at St. Thomas, Valverde preceded him to the Venezuelan capital. In the politically chaotic atmosphere of Caracas, Valverde publically proclaimed his own status as that of a "secret agent," at once raising doubts as to the authenticity of Duarte's credentials and destroying the favorable impression the Venezuelans then had of the new regime in Santo Domingo. Duarte continued to negotiate patiently and with tact, but the arrival of still another Minister Plenipotentiary, Candelario Oquendo, made his position untenable. Duarte wrote a letter to the provisional government, begging them to stop spending money and sending agents abroad, but the damage had been done. The foreign press, influenced by Spanish propaganda, reported that the Dominican Republic was not undergoing a struggle for independence, but rather a civil war between utopian idealists, self-seekers, and partisans of annexation to France, the United States, and Spain. There was sufficient truth in this claim and in the shocking news that the Dominicans were now putting their negotiations with Spain in the hands of the president of Haiti, to convince Duarte at last that his mission was hopeless. If the Dominican Republic refused to be truly independent, if it persisted in ignominiously attaching itself to the tail of any one of these imperialistic kites, he wanted no part of the perfidy. "If our country," he wrote, "shall not sail free and independent *of all foreign power,* it must sink."

Giving up any thought of returning home and contributing, even so much as by an expression of disgust, to the fratricidal division of his country, Duarte now retired into complete obscurity. His last years in exile were spent in extreme poverty. Friendless and forgotten, he died in Caracas at the age of sixty-three on July 15, 1876.

In his romanticism, in his religious character, and especially in his naïve belief that the force of nationalism alone would be enough to overcome the habits of sloth, venality, and moral decay brought on by tyranny, Duarte was the child of his time. But in the selflessness with which he pursued his ideal, and in his lifelong refusal to compromise with any of those adventurers bent upon perverting patriotic fervor into personal aggrandizement, Duarte stands out above his time—or any time. Almost a hundred years after his death, when his country lay prostrate under a far more pervasive tyranny than any he had known, it was Duarte's spirit that would give courage to a new conspiracy for freedom, and that would look down in the years to come, in peace or in anguish, upon the destination of Quisqueya's bounty.

V

"*Tweedledum*" and "*Tweedledee*," *1845-60*

Personal Rule under the Alternating Piracies of Santana and Baez

In pursuing the career of Juan Pablo Duarte to its tragic close, we left Pedro Santana and Buenaventura Baez at the opening of the year 1845 with the fate of the infant republic in their hands. Never has a weak charge been left to such guardians. The atmosphere was noxious. The prescriptions were lethal. The infanticides were heartless—and brazen. If the Dominican state survived, it was not because Santana and Baez had neglected any opportunity to sell its enfeebled body to the highest bidder. But the bidders themselves fell apart over the chance to get something for nothing; and the victim, even at death's door, showed remarkable recuperative powers.

Identical twins in so far as their shameless ability to survive revelations of treachery was concerned, the two *caudillos* of 1845-60 were deceptively dissimilar in personality and appearance. Santana—burly, brutish and brave—had all the virtues and defects of a small-town self-made man. Lacking principles and intelligence, he was always able to exert his simple animal magnetism and effectively command when mere survival was at stake; and equally able, when

59

wisdom and magnanimity were required in the intervals of "peace," to identify the advancement of his personal fortunes with those of the state. When the state showed signs of crumbling, Santana was always quick to retire, with the cunning of a beast, to the lair of his luxurious *estancia,* "El Prado" near Seybo. When opportunity for another foray beckoned, he would emerge, hastily replenish his coffers, and retire again with a grimace of puzzled wonderment at the ingratitude of the "fickle" masses or "self-seeking" civilians who were forcing him to relinquish the helm again to his more guileful opposite number.

It is remarkable that no one has drawn a parallel between Pedro Santana and Mexico's jack-in-the-box dictator of the same epoch, Antonio Lopez de Santa Anna, whose very name has an identical ring. Like his equally brave Dominican counterpart, Santa Anna made an honorable name for himself in his country's first struggle for independence, only to squander it in a series of eight bouts with the presidency, replete with raids on the treasury, comic opera "defenses" of freedom, resounding titles, and periodic retirements in high dudgeon to "Manga de Clavo," a fat *hacienda* hard by the bemedaled general's "Seybo"—Vera Cruz. And like Don Pedro in Hispaniola, Don Antonio finally crowned his infamous career by bartering his very country (one half of which he sacrificed quite needlessly to the United States) for the discharge of a personal vendetta and a final shot at meaningless rule. "Manga de Clavo," Santa Anna's Sybaritic estate, and Don Pedro's "El Prado" have both vanished from the face of the earth without leaving a trace, but the heritage of the one, who amused himself with his fighting cocks, and the other, who swung in his hammock observing the increase of his herds of cattle and hogs, survive in the ruthless greed of less gaudy politicians to plague their respective countries.

Buenaventura Baez, the suave, imperturbable, no-face intriguer, with his cold, blue eyes and frizzly "Burnsides," was a figure less admirable and more clever than either. Lacking Don Pedro's capacity to make peasants follow him into battle or cheer him in a Roman triumph, as well as Don Antonio's engaging sensuality and flair for the melodramatic, Baez was able at one and the same time to play with consummate skill on the patriotic sentimentality of the masses, the obsessive fear for his job of the petty bureaucrat, and the chronic insecurity of the money-hungry tradesman. The great abolitionist Charles Sumner once described Baez as being "uncertain of opinions, without character, without patriotism, without truth, looking out supremely for himself, and on any side according to imagined self-interest." Loading his soft-spoken oratory with false promises, Baez balanced the greedy maneuvers of one great power against another in order to be thrown a jackal's share of whichever one might come up with the loot. Yet Baez had an altogether fantastic ability to make men forget his wolfish acts of yesterday or be persuaded that the wolf's clothes (reversing the proverb) contained a sheep. Born in 1810 to a mulatto slave girl in the family of the Spanish priest and author Don Antonio Sánchez Valverde, Baez used the paternal estate of Azua as his base of operations, but never as his refuge. He was a man of the world in the worst sense of the phrase, educated abroad, and willing to serve any race or nation that would pay him for the privilege. He glided between the courts of Spain, France, England, Haiti, and the United States with all the natural inconspicuousness of a chameleon, returning home, when opportunity knocked, to seize power with all the dignity of a toad.

It is hardly surprising that during the Haitian occupation of his country in the last years of Boyer, Buenaventura Baez had been happy to serve in various offices under the Haitian government. And indeed, which representing the province of Azua in Port-au-Prince, he had intrigued *against* Haiti with the French envoy—not with the object of freeing his own land, but of making it a French protectorate. In fact, the only curious thing about this, or about Baez' subsequent action in sending a secret emissary to Port-au-Prince to inform the Haitian president of the "Trinitarios'" movements, is that these treacheries never became political liabilities in Baez' subsequent career.

In the early days of the struggle for independence, Baez and Santana cooperated amicably. Santana's failure to follow up, after his victory over the Haitians at Baní, was in accord with the French desire to weaken the provisional government so much that only a protectorate might save it. Santana admitted as much in a letter to the junta president, Bobadilla, a former Boyer aide: "The longer the struggle lasts the more uncertain becomes the victory . . . [thus insuring] *the triumph of our policy.*" And it was no accident that when the people began to get wind of this counterrevolutionary plot, Bobadilla, Baez, and the others were permitted to escape by Francisco del Rosario Sánchez, whose allegiance to Duarte was already wavering and who was later to intrigue in Haiti against the independence of his country.

We have already observed Santana's refusal to relinquish his command and his march upon the capital, terminating in the arrest of the "Trinitarios." The powerless junta was permitted to draw up a constitution, along the lines of the American one, but that was the last of its acts. Santana refused to govern without dictatorial powers, whereupon Article 210, granting him such powers "temporarily," was inserted; and on November 13, 1844, the dictator took the oath of office at San Cristobal and became first president of the Republic.

Santana's first term in power (1844-48) was fairly uneventful. The paternalistic ruler established courts under the Napoleonic code, imposed curfews, ordained strict work codes, granted high salaries to himself and his staff, printed paper money to pay off the standing army, and executed several batches of conspirators suspected of hatching plots to unseat him. After failing to gain American recognition—though Secretary of State Calhoun of South Carolina toyed with the idea of a joint Spanish-French-American backing to prevent the further spread of Negro influence in the Caribbean—Santana dispatched Baez to Spain to seek a protectorate there. Spain, which had been vastly relieved to surrender its neglected, unproductive colony fifty years before, was not interested. So long as Paris, London, and Washington were too busy elsewhere to intervene in Dominican affairs themselves, Madrid was perfectly willing to let matters drift.

On August 4, 1848, as an easy way of avoiding another anticipated coup (this on the part of his underlings), Santana turned over the government to the most vociferous of them, his war minister Manuel Jiménez, and withdrew to "El Prado." Jiménez, weak and incompetent, was thus described in a diplomatic report to Washington the following year:

> His whole time was spent in cleaning, training, and fighting cocks, it being frequently necessary to send acts of Congress and other official papers to the cock-pit for his approval and signature. Under his rule, everything fell into confusion, which state of things was soon made known to Soulouque and incited him to the invasion of the Republic.

Who was Soulouque? It is related that President Boyer of Haiti, once lecturing his mulatto staff about the dangers of instability, pointed to a soldier dozing in a hammock and remarked that at such a time "any man in Haiti might become president, even that stupid Negro over there." Years later, in 1847, when the mulattoes and blacks could not agree on a candidate, they turned to Faustin Soulouque (still in his hammock) and made him their compromise figurehead. Soulouque, it seems, had only been playing dead. Not only did he "retire" the mulatto caste to commercial status, answering their one effort to resume control with a bloodbath; he set up an efficient secret police (ancestor of President François Duvalier's present-day *Tontons-Macoutes*), gave a free hand in the religious field to the voodoo priests, and after creating a hereditary black aristocracy of four princes, fifty-nine dukes, and several hundred lesser noblemen of the blood, had himself crowned emperor, with the logical and impressive title Faustin I.

For the ten years of his nightmarish reign, Soulouque attempted to distract attention from the graft and economic havoc he was creating at home by mounting periodic invasions of his neighbor. Fortunately for the Dominicans (the emperor had sworn not to leave so much as a fighting cock alive across the border), the invading armies were without spirit, and most incompetently led; but unfortunately for the Dominicans, the constant threat thus posed played into the hands of their own tormentors, Santana and Baez. The invasion of 1849 was stemmed by volunteer forces under the patriots Ramón Mella and Duvergé, but the *coup de grâce* to the onrushing horde was delivered at Las Carreras by Santana, who had been hastily recalled from his retreat in Seybo by the panicky capital—at the instigation of Buenaventura Baez.

Baez was "elected" to his first term as president on September 24, not because the victorious Santana wished to pay a debt, but because he had failed to get an honest liberal (Santiago Espaillat) to assume the puppetship, and because he thought that with Baez' schemes for a French protectorate forced into the glare of official publicity, his chief rival would be hoist by his own petard. Accepting the generalship of the armed forces and the title "Liberator of the Fatherland," Santana resumed his observation post at "El Prado" and waited.

After announcing a thoroughgoing series of domestic reforms which he had no intention of forcing beyond the paper stage, Baez settled down to his lifelong business—the securing of a foreign protectorate which would insure his own perpetuation close to the moneybags. Imperialistic Americans, now encouraged by the ease with which Mexico under Santa Anna had surrendered half her territory to the United States, were close to persuading their weak president, Zachary Taylor, that annexation of the Dominican Republic would be the best way of forestalling the ambitions of the European powers. The American agent to Santo Domingo, Benjamin Green, reported back to Washington:

England, France desire above all things to get possession of Samaná. . . .
This Government will not hesitate to grant it for a term of years or in

perpetuity to whichever will negotiate and guarantee a treaty of peace with Haiti so as to enable them to go to work and recover from the poverty to which the long war has reduced them. I have no doubt that they would prefer to make such an arrangement with the United States. . . . I have to request that you inform me by the earliest opportunity how far our Government will be willing to interfere between this Government and Haiti to bring about that result by negotiation or otherwise, and whether, if offered to me, I may accept Samaná as a consideration for our giving notice to the Haitians that they must cease to molest this people.

While France stalled over Baez' inquiries, Great Britain got into the act by making it clear to both France and the United States that she would seize Samaná rather than see it turned over to the French as a consideration for free trade and a loan to clinch Baez' tobacco monopoly. The United States turned to Santana in the hope of frustrating the Francophile Baez, but Buenaventura, ever ready to find a more effective backer, requested that the United States intervene to prevent a second invasion by Soulouque. By this time Soulouque had made his terms known. In return for Haitian sovereignty over the whole island, he would be glad to confer titles of nobility on Santana, Baez, and their friends, the former to be appointed military commandant of the eastern "provinces," the latter civil commissioner.

The British ambassador to Santo Domingo, meanwhile, not disdaining to trade on the circumstance of Baez' mixed blood by reminding him that the United States oppressed Negroes and mulattoes alike, made temporary common cause with the French. But the Americans, at the insistence of Daniel Webster who had just been appointed Secretary of State by President Taylor's more competent successor, immediately joined the French and British in insisting that Emperor Faustin declare a truce. Truce was declared, but since it became perfectly clear that Soulouque had no intention of giving permanent guarantees and that to count on the permanent restraining hand of the three bickering rival powers would be equally folly, Baez made a halfhearted attempt to mobilize a new citizens' army. Clearly the time had come for Santana to re-emerge from "El Prado."

On February 15, 1853, Don Pedro took the presidency again with the following ringing exhortation to national unity:

> Dominicans! I was in retirement in my home given up to the care of my family and enjoying, moreover, the tranquillity which has been existing for some time in our beloved country, when the voice of the people, which is for me the first of all laws, called me by suffrage to preside for the fourth time over the destinies of the Nation. . . . I value justly the helpful influence which the intervention of powerful friendly nations can exert over the destinies of the Republic in their decision to protect our sacred cause by intimating to the Haitian Government that it must cease in its impudent and impracticable pretensions to dominate this territory.
> . . .
> Long live religion, national union, independence and the Dominican Republic!

After receiving the congratulations of Francisco del Rosario Sánchez, sending General Ramón Mella on a futile mission to Spain, and offering the War Ministry to Duarte's betrayer of 1843, Felipe Alfáu, Santana proceeded with the blackening of Baez' already tarnished reputation. This he accomplished easily by disclosing for the first time publicly Baez' complicity with the Haitians in opposing independence and his subsequent treasonable negotiations with Port-au-Prince and Paris. Baez, who had already fled to St. Thomas, replied logically enough, asking why, if Santana had been aware of his alleged treason for so many years, he had appointed him president? But to defend himself against the charges themselves—an impossibility—Baez said not a word.

Spurned by Spain and aware that France's solicitude for Baez was only the by-product of her determination to keep Haiti solvent enough to continue paying the installments on Boyer's fantastic promissory note, Santana turned once more to the United States.

Franklin Pierce, the fourteenth American president, though he was nominally a Jacksonian liberal and had had his campaign biography written by Nathaniel Hawthorne, fell in easily with the expansionist fervor then gripping American business. Pierce had fought under Scott in Mexico. Now he added to America's Mexican acquisitions through the Gadsden Purchase. He opposed the antislavery agitation of the abolitionists, and he recognized the outright piracy of the filibuster William Walker in Nicaragua. It was inevitable that he should send an agent to Santo Domingo; and when the agent informed him that there were unlimited "concessions" available to the "manifest destiny" of the United States—in mining, salt, timber, railroads, public utilities—and that Santana's continuance in office would make seizing these easy, he naturally turned an interested ear. The result was the drafting of a commercial treaty. In return for favorable credit arrangements, the Dominican government was to give the United States a square mile of strategic Samaná Peninsula on which to erect a coaling depot at an annual rental fee of three hundred dollars. All might have gone well with this nefarious deal except that Captain George B. McClellan, later to achieve dubious fame as one of Lincoln's ill-fated commanders, made an enthusiastically premature survey of Samaná, thus playing into the hands of Santana's political foes. France and England, alerted, insinuated to Santana in no uncertain terms that should he go through with his American deal, the Haitians would immediately be unleashed upon him. Santana backed down, agreeing to a more modest treaty, but even this he was not permitted to submit to his congress since the British and French sent war vessels to Santo Domingo, and the British Ambassador with unlimited effrontery visited the provinces to "inform" the Dominican people that ratification would be followed by enslavement to the United States.

Emperor Faustin, meanwhile, heartened by these rebuffs to Santana administered by his French and English "friends" and determined to put an end once and for all to the possibility that the slaveholding United States might take over Hispaniola, launched his last invasion. It began in the last days of November, 1855. Santana, who had retreated into his shell, as always when the subtleties of civilian rule became too much for him, bounced back to the helm with alacrity. He was in his element. Veterans and volunteers responded. At two battles on December 22 the Emperor's undisciplined horde was routed. The victory of Santomé in the south under Santana's personal command was the decisive one.

His hands now freed by these triumphs, Santana at once signed the revised treaty with the United States, though he decided to let the controversial matter of the Samaná "rental" wait until later. France and England, roused anew by this hint that the United States might be securing a bridgehead accessible to the eventual annexations of Cuba and Puerto Rico, now found a ready partner in Spain. The Spanish Consul was instructed to first mollify Santana by presenting him with a medal and a renunciation of all Spain's former rights in the colony. But when Santana failed to be impressed by this belated and barefaced attempt to make up for leaving the Dominicans to their fate when the Haitians poured in—Santana contemptuously sent a deputy to accept the decoration for him—the Spanish representative availed himself of the only remaining, and obvious, alternative. He turned to Buenaventura Baez.

Baez was still in exile, of course, but his partisans had been slipping back into Santo Domingo one by one and were already active. The audacious and impudent Spanish Consul proceeded to invoke an ambiguous clause in the Dominican constitution and for two dollars a head began to register Dominicans ("for their future protection") as Spanish citizens! Santana's prestige from his military successes was still great, and he could easily have called Spain's bluff by putting an end to this provocative meddling in Dominican affairs, but, disheartened by the American coolness which followed his postponement of the Samaná question and remembering the speed with which his countrymen had always recalled him after earlier manifestations of "ingratitude," he decided to sulk in his tent again, retiring to "El Prado."

Baez, in St. Thomas since 1852, returned like a homing pigeon. Eased back into office as vice president under Santana's hand-picked successor, General Regla Mota, he quickly secured the adhesion of the French and British representatives to the intrigue of the Spanish

Consul, and on December 8, 1856, successfully maneuvered Mota's resignation and his own reinstallation in the presidential chair.

If Baez now embarked upon a stern and forthright opposition to American imperialism, it is not to be thought for a moment that this worthy policy was dictated by any concern for Dominican independence or that he could not pursue an exactly opposite course (as indeed he soon would) once circumstances changed. For the present, he ostentatiously built fortifications to repel an "imminent" American naval attack and at a diplomatic reception righteously refused to toast "the President of the Filibusterers." This done, he proceeded to the elimination of his old enemy, Santana. The Liberator, he intoned, was "a despot who by his own acts has placed himself without the law." But before making this bold *démarche,* Baez was careful to protect his flanks by replacing Santana's followers in public office with members of his own prolific family and sealing off the old man's escape hatches in the Seybo. In January of 1857 Santana was arrested at "El Prado," placed aboard a French vessel, and shipped, appropriately enough, to St. Thomas.

Baez' fourth term in office lasted less than two years. Spain unexpectedly recalled its conniving consul from Santo Domingo, and nothing Baez could do to return him to favor succeeded. The printing of quantities of paper money, which Baez' henchmen acquired at cut rates to buy up the lucrative tobacco crop in the Cibao, caused economic ruin in that area. In no time at all the leaders of the Cibao had raised an army and were marching on the capital. Had these rebels stood behind the liberal constitution they drew up in Santiago on February 19, 1858—and behind its author, the statesmanlike Ulises Espaillat—something constructive might have come out of this rebellion. But when Santana returned to the Republic and took charge of the troops besieging the capital, the result was predictable. The siege, accompanied by starvation and pestilence, dragged on because the Baecistas were afraid to surrender to their merciless enemy. Mediation was finally undertaken by the commanding officer of an American naval vessel. Under the terms of this arrangement, Baez and his gang were permitted to take ship to Curaçao, and Santana undertook to govern with moderation.

Santana's conception of how to govern, moderately or otherwise, never changed. Surrounding himself, as he had during his two previous regimes, with those cronies who had helped him get rid of Duarte, he proceeded to liquidate the new liberal party in the Cibao. No attempt whatever was made to alleviate the misery of the people, now separated from the remnants of their foreign trade by the depreciation of Baez' worthless *papeletas*. The overthrow of Faustin Soulouque in Haiti by General Fabre Geffrard freed Santana's hands momentarily for the undertaking of his lifelong ambition—a foreign protectorate that would at once guarantee the Republic against further Haitian incursions and at the same time perpetuate his own "do nothing" rule. Cleverly putting France and England off guard by giving them lucrative concessions in timber and minerals, and at the same time dispatching an envoy to Washington to negotiate a new commercial treaty there, Santana sent Felipe Alfáu to Spain to find out for him once and for all whether there were any terms under which the monarchy would consent to assume responsibility for the now totally bankrupt Republic.

VI

Insurrections Unlimited, 1861-78

Annexation by Spain and the Wars of the Restoration

On March 17, 1861, the citizens of Santo Domingo woke up to find the walls and billboards of the capital plastered with proclamations commanding them to assemble in the cathedral square the following day. When they began arriving, General Santana, recently given dictatorial powers by the senate, appeared on the gallery of the Palace of Justice with the members of his government. After the reading of a document announcing the reincorporation of the country into the Spanish dominions, the red and gold flag of Spain was raised on the fort and on the "Puerto del Conde" and greeted with a 101-gun salute. Three days later the event was interpreted for the people in an editorial in the first issue of the new royal *Gaceta* as follows:

> Long live the Queen!
> The glorious Spanish flag, that symbol of civilization which for more than three centuries waved over our towers and fortresses, has been raised again in this Antillean Island favored by Isabel I, loved by Columbus, and from now on under the protection of Isabel II, the Magnanimous, today once more our august sovereign.

As the result of this event the Dominican people have seen the realization of their most fervent hopes and of their most real and noble aspirations and in truth, the act in which there took place the solemn proclamation of our political transfer could not have been more spontaneous nor could have satisfied more fully the sincere desires of this people.

. . . His Excellency (Santana) presented himself on the principal balcony of the Palace of Justice, from which, as the result of the frank and spontaneous expression of the will of the people and of the infinite number of petitions which the people had sent him, declaring himself definitely in favor of the incorporation of this part of the Island in the Spanish Monarchy, he addressed in a loud and clear voice to his fellow-citizens a fervent allocution. . . .

Thus has been briefly indicated the manner in which our political transfer has been effected, a unique example in the history of other countries, but not so in our country which has already given to all unique examples of perfect fidelity and love at all periods, and which, far from being led astray by false illusions, sees and feels the reality of things. . . .

The allocution of Santana, read to a score of similar gatherings in the principal towns of the country, was, if anything, even more mendacious, hypocritical, and unctuous:

Dominicans! It is not many years since that my loyal and consistent voice reminded you, in presenting to you the reform of our political constitution, in these words, "Our national glories, the heritage of the great and noble people to whom we owe our origin."

In making them so truly manifest my sentiments, I thought as well that I was the faithful interpreter of your own, and indeed I was not mistaken. My own policy was then forever indicated, but your own has gone even further than my fondest hopes believed.

Many and spontaneous petitions of the people have come to my hands, and if, yesterday, you had granted me extraordinary powers, today you yourselves are hoping that that which your loyalty has ever desired may indeed become fact. Religion, language, beliefs and customs, all we maintain unaltered. Not, however, that there have not been those who have attempted to take from us such precious gifts; and the nation which has given us so much is the same nation which today is bending its arms like a loving mother who recovers her child lost in the shipwreck in which its brothers have perished.

Dominicans! Only the ambition and resentment of one man [Baez] have alienated us from our mother country. . . .

I, who realize how urgent are your needs, wish you to hear the Spanish Nation and look well at what she offers us.

She grants us the civil liberty which her own people enjoy and guarantees to us our personal liberty and therefore removes the danger of our losing it; she assures to us our prosperity, recognizing as valid all the acts of the Republic; she offers to bear in mind and to reward all cases of merit and will not forget services which have been devoted to the country; finally, she brings peace to this soil where so many combats have taken place, and with peace she brings the benefits of peace. . . .

Readers who have followed the annexationist machinations of Santana and Baez thus far will not be surprised at this sudden consummation, but they may be curious to know the train of events that led up to it. On March 5, 1859, Santana had attempted to revive his lifeless treasury by offering to redeem Baez' almost worthless *papeletas* at a little more than their current market rate—two thousand to one Spanish dollar. The consuls of Spain, France, and England, seeing their chance to speculate vanishing, demanded insolently that the rate of exchange be raised—or else. After trying vainly to get the American commercial agent, Jonathan Elliott, to join them in this highhanded ultimatum, they asked for their passports and left the country. On November 30 the consuls returned—on warships dispatched by their respective countries.

Santana and Baez had meanwhile been preparing for this eventuality in their separate fashions. Baez, in Curaçao, had directed his partisans in the Republic—now headed by Francisco del Rosario Sánchez and working closely with President Geffrard of Haiti—to incite insurrections against Santana; two of these were suppressed by General Abad Alfáu, following which the principal conspirators were exiled. Santana, meanwhile, having retired prudently to "El Prado" to await the outcome of these incitements from abroad, had sent Felipe Alfáu to Spain again to seek the best possible terms. The first intimation that these negotiations in Madrid were bearing fruit was that the Spanish Consul suddenly withdrew from the menacing

front of the big powers. Santana appeared to yield to the continued
insistence of France and England that he "meet his obligations,"
but letters from Madrid were already in his hands guaranteeing
that Spain rather than the Dominican Republic would inherit the
consequences.

The American agent, General William Cazneau of Texas, was
all this while doing his unscrupulous best to turn Santana's difficul-
ties in a direction favorable to annexationist sentiment in Washington. James Buchanan, Pierce's honest and equally weak successor,
was already on record (as a cosigner of the famous Ostend Manifesto) as favoring a containment of antislavery forces in the Caribbean. Cuba, the Manifesto had declared, should be "bought" from
Spain, and if Spain refused to sell, taken forcibly: "We should be
unworthy of our gallant forefathers, and commit base treason
against our posterity, should we permit Cuba to be Africanized and
become a second Santo Domingo, with all its attendant horrors to
the white race. . . ." The Democratic party under Buchanan was ready
to go to almost any lengths to placate the southern slave states, and
Cazneau very cleverly couched his plea for annexation thus:

> The Baez party which aims at placing the supreme control in the
> hands of the negroes, was defeated and driven from the City in July,
> 1858, after sustaining a siege of eleven months. Its leaders relied on the
> sympathy of England and France. . . . At present the Cabinet, Congress
> and Courts are filled by white men. . . . The restoration of Baez or the
> annexation to Haiti, strongly but secretly urged by France and England,
> would sweep them out en masse to be replaced by blacks selected from
> the class most bitterly opposed to American interests.

Probably nothing less than the imminence of civil war at home
prevented Buchanan from acting upon this and more urgent pleas
for intervention. Cazneau had commercial interests in Santo Domingo
to protect, and as he realized which way the wind was blowing, he
began to minimize Santana's negotiations with Spain in his reports
to Washington, at the same time going out of his way to blacken

the reputation of Jonathan Elliott, the American commercial agent, whom he accused of both drunkenness and "incitement of the colored class against the government." It was no wonder that Santana's domestic foes could make small headway. Sánchez in St. Thomas, already discredited by his Haitian intrigues, could be ignored. The patriot Ramón Mella protested and was promptly imprisoned. Don Fernando Arturo de Meriño, vicar-general of the Church, had the courage to proclaim at a *Te Deum* that "True patriotism is the first of a citizen's duties," but by this time (February 27, 1861) Santana and Baez had so confused the minds of the citizens regarding the proper object of a citizen's loyalty that it was too late.

Early in April of 1861 the Secretary of State to the new American President, Abraham Lincoln, directed a memorandum to the White House entitled "Some Thoughts for the President's Consideration." The gist of William H. Seward's attempt to divert his chief's attention from slavery and secession was this: warn France and Spain to desist from their violations of the Monroe Doctrine in Mexico and the Dominican Republic; if they fail to respond to this ultimatum "convene Congress and declare war against them."

The Dominican Republic was not to be so easily released from its new bondage; like Mexico it would have to dispose of its Maximilians by its own efforts. Lincoln refused to be diverted. On April 12 Fort Sumter was attacked, igniting the American Civil War. Seward's memorandum was leaked to the press and its publication so infuriated the European imperialists that they took sides throughout the conflict with the Confederacy. And in Spain itself, under the leadership of the Napoleonic soldier and conqueror of Morocco, Henry Joseph O'Donnell, the old fantasy of a return to imperial glory through fresh foreign acquisitions began to burn brightly for the last time.

If ever a colonial power was given the kind of chance history so

seldom offers to profit from the mistakes of the past, it was Spain.
Under O'Donnell a measure of stability and prosperity was found,
but in 1863 O'Donnell's Union-Liberal ministry was overthrown
and the traditional political incapacity of the Spaniards reasserted
itself. The attempt of Queen Isabella II to rule despotically through
a group of incompetent bedfellows whose murderous intrigues became the scandal of Europe, insured that colonial administration
would sink to new depths of unprincipled corruption.

Even in the first years of the annexation, while O'Donnell was
still in power and his viceroys, Serraño in Cuba and Peláez in Santo
Domingo, were making some effort to win the consent of the
governed, signs of failure became manifest. At the time of the ceremonial take over, popular indifference had been sufficiently widespread to make opposition to Santana's coup unlikely. Santana
cynically explained the reason to a Spaniard in the capital: "I have
made you an immensely valuable gift, for I have given you a people
without journalists and devoid of lawyers." If the small percentage
of literate Dominicans had found an honest spokesman, there was
no forum in which he could have addressed them, no courts beyond
the jurisdiction of Santana's sycophants. O'Donnell had insisted
that annexation must be preceded by "unanimous consent," but the
belated way in which Santana had gone about delivering this consent—at carefully stage-managed ceremonials, without alternatives,
without submission to legislative bodies or courts—perfectly fore-
shadowed the rigged elections stage-managed by Trujillo in the century to follow:

> The Proclamation is to be made immediately; the Spanish flag is to be
> raised; a solemn notarial act of the ceremony is to be written, which must
> be signed by all the people present who know how to write, and the
> names of the persons who do not know how to write are to be included
> in it. . . . As soon as the flag has been saluted with twenty-one guns, the
> "comandantes de armas" are to be notified. . . . The Proclamation should
> be made as early as possible in the morning, so that the Dominican flag
> need not be raised. . . . A Te Deum is to be sung and the civil governor

of the Province is to address an allocution to the public, to explain the guarantees and the advantages which the annexation implies. . . .

What did it take for even the illiterate to become aware that they were being manipulated? Much less than the evidence of their eyes and ears. Hordes of Spanish soldiers were now garrisoned in the towns—six thousand from Cuba and Puerto Rico had been landed by midsummer of 1861. Hundreds of imported petty officials had supplanted the native bureaucrats, and at greatly increased salaries. Spanish priests were introducing a note of unprecedented intolerance into parish affairs. The promise to redeem the paper money with gold or silver had not been kept. "Reform" of the tariff was strangling trade, benefiting only Spanish explorers. A little more than six weeks after the Proclamation of Annexation, the first organized revolts had broken out.

Now came another of those splendid opportunities for genuine Haitian-Dominican *rapprochement* that always seemed to founder in a morass of misinterpreted motives. This one was no exception. President Geffrard had been giving refuge and even financial encouragement to the guerilla bands along the border under the leadership of Generals Sánchez and José María Cabral. It could be argued that Geffrard supported them only because they aimed to return the unscrupulous Baez to power and that a neighbor constantly torn asunder by such as Baez and Santana was bound to be a weak neighbor. Patriots of both countries, however, had everything to lose from the return of an imperialist power to Hispaniola. Geffrard, who might have united the independents of both peoples against intervention from abroad, allowed himself to be intimidated by Spain. Sánchez was lured into ambush and executed without trial by Santana. And when a Spanish fleet anchored off Port-au-Prince, the frightened Haitian ruler not only guaranteed to patrol the boundary henceforth, but to pay an indemnity of $200,000.

Santana must now have regretted the good old days when he could blame bad times on his political foes and retire to "El Prado."

Now he could only show his growing resentment over Spain's broken promises by swinging petulantly in his hammock while Serraño, the captain-general of Cuba just disembarked on a state visit, was being offered a *Te Deum* in the cathedral a block away. Serraño placated the surly captain-general of Santo Domingo by calling on him in his home and promising that Spain would reverse its policy in the matter of giving the high-paying jobs to Santana's friends, but the old *caudillo* went to receive the Knight's Grand Cross of the American Order of Isabel la Católica "barefoot and clad only in a shirt and linen pantaloons."

On March 28, 1862, hoping to arrest the increasing contempt shown for his authority, Santana resigned as captain-general. His resignation was unexpectedly accepted. Granted the title Marqués de las Carreras and a life pension of $12,000, he retired once again to his *estancia* in the Seybo. Grievances against Spain's autocratic rule had come to the point where even Santana could see no hope of resisting the inevitable. The military, their top commissions taken over by Spanish officers, were beginning to look to the disaffected provinces for hopes of a comeback. Santana's ousted friends in the civil service were howling for redress. Even Baecistas were moving into their old jobs. When Spain finally did get around to redeeming the Dominican *papeletas* (with paper of worse quality), the entire issue of $50 notes was without justification declared counterfeit. Merchants and big farmers faced ruin. Disastrous tax levies completed it. The substitution of the medieval Spanish penal code for the more enlightened Napoleonic one caused further unrest. The new Spanish archbishop not only annulled freedom of worship, destroying the Methodists and threatening the Masonic Order to which Santana himself belonged, but, by abolishing fees for parochial services, reduced the native priests to beggary and turned them into archenemies of Spain.

When an outbreak of yellow fever, the same dread affliction that had defeated Leclerc's army in Haiti sixty-five years before, began to decimate the Spanish garrison, the opposition took heart and began to agitate openly. By the end of September, things had gone so far that Governor-General Rivera secretly advised the court to abandon the island. But unfortunately for Spain and for its ill-fated "colony," politics would not permit the politicians to withdraw gracefully. A most devastating two years of combat lay ahead.

In April of 1863 an insurrection in the Cibao under General Lucas de Peña was defeated by the better armed Spanish troops. In August, Generals Pedro Pimentel and Benito Monción took charge of much more widespread uprisings in the north, and with the help of a Haitian guerilla leader opposing President Geffrard established border "sanctuaries" valuable to both. The Spaniards were now on the horns of a dilemma. If they acted alone, they but confirmed the necessity of Monción's slogan, "Liberty or death, and a war of extermination to all Spaniards and their blood." If they called upon Santana—but how could they call upon the very man they had rebuked for treating earlier rebels too brutally? Yet someone had to be called to the rescue, and who but the indomitable Marqués de las Carreras? Santana was indomitable enough, even in his old age, but it had been one thing to raise levies of patriots to stem hordes of Haitian marauders; it was quite another to have to cool one's heels in the viceroy's antechamber waiting for reinforcements of mercenaries to shoot down one's own people. And when they did arrive, Santana marched north by way of Monte Plata to find that the army of occupation there had lost six thousand rifles to the rebels and been forced to flee in disorder, that patriots had not hesitated to burn Santiago and Puerto Plata to the ground, that virtually every town and hamlet in the land was openly declaring for a new provisional government.

The rebel union was established in September of 1863. We have already seen, in relating the melancholy history of Duarte's last visit to his homeland, how Espaillat, Mella, and the other liberals who formed this provisional regime soon succumbed to the pragmatic politics of the soldiers. In the final months of 1863, Spain made a belated effort to restore its prestige by withdrawing the pro-consuls who had committed undeniable crimes; but this policy, and halfhearted attempts to negotiate with the provisional government, only served to infuriate Santana. Reverting to habit, he began to issue his own orders. On Christmas Day the provisional government declared the "Liberator" guilty of high treason and orders were issued to track him down and shoot him on sight.

Still stalled at Monte Plata on his march to the Cibao, Santana's dwindling forces were systematically whittled away by the provisional government's brilliant Negro captain from Puerto Plata, Gregorio Luperón. Santana's oldest confederates began to desert him. The Spanish high command in the capital lost confidence in him. Reinforcements no longer arrived. Forced to evacuate Monte Plata, the old general with the remnants of his troops was now pushed back into the Seybo. In May of 1864 La Gándara, the new Spanish captain-general, ordered Santana to accept Spanish direction entirely or face court-martial. The old man, infirm and bedridden, penned a last letter to his alien masters, charging them (not illogically) with base ingratitude. Then, making a supreme effort, Santana undertook his final journey from "El Prado" to the capital. What must have passed through his mind as he approached Santo Domingo on June 13 is cogently surmised by Sumner Welles:

> The long years when the Haitians ruled over the land, and the secret conspiracies in which he had so often taken part; the first call to arms when he had collected about him his loyal farmers from the Seybo to march to Azua; the intrigues of Baez; the steady growth of the ambition which tormented him more and more as the years passed by—the vision of a foreign Power which would guard his country and permit him, so long as life would last, to remain the supreme authority; the glories of Azua and Las Carreras, and the cheering crowds as he rode back to the capital so many times at the head of his victorious army; where were those now who had applauded him then? Instead of being the supreme power, the hero of his country, the Liberator of the Fatherland, he was execrated, detested by them all, an outlaw for whose assassination any patriot would receive the thanks of the Dominican people, a defeated subordinate broken by the Spanish Captain-General.

Santana's sudden death on June 14, by stroke or by suicide, removed the last fiction of Dominican acquiescence in Spain's presence.
From now on the army of occupation would have to annihilate its
unwilling hosts or get out. The pigheaded La Gándara was determined to carry on against all obstacles, but four circumstances combined to make impossible his strategy of holding the southern and
northern ports while starving out the rebels in the Cibao.

First, Spain had already lost half of the twenty thousand men
she had thrown into the holding operation. A thousand had fallen
in battle; nine thousand had succumbed to fevers and smallpox, and
the incidence of disease was rising. The ships dispatched from Cuba
to blockade the northern harbors were rotten. Some had burned-out
boilers. One was so far gone that when it fired a salute in the harbor
of Port-au-Prince its sides caved in and it had to be towed back to
Spain.

Second, those veterans who could be landed to take the offensive
in the interior—reinforced by green Dominican auxiliaries con-
scripted in violation of the annexation agreement—were no match
for the guerillas of Luperón and Pimentel. Anyone who has attempted
to cross the towering coastal range that lies between Santiago and
Puerto Plata, even in a car, or braved the cactus jungle between
Guayubín and Monción, will readily understand that all the advantages must go with the defense.

The characteristically ambiguous foreign policy of the United
States—failing to recognize its democratic friends but at the same
time giving them arms and covert commercial arrangements—was
not helping Spain. When the Confederacy collapsed early in 1865,
it became perfectly obvious that the American government would
resume its piecemeal elimination of European interference in Latin
American affairs.

Fourth, the downfall of O'Donnell's Liberal Union in Spain led
to an immediate reappraisal of the dreams of colonial glory on
which it had been based. The new government headed by the Duke
of Valencia turned over the Dominican fiasco to the Cortes, and

the Cortes voted to get out despite Serraño's plea "to save the nation's honor and the future of Spain's West Indian colonies."

The decision to evacuate might have been carried out gracefully but for the spite of La Gándara—and the instability of the provisional government. On March 25 a new constitutional government was formed to replace the provisional government which had been overthrown by a rebellion in January. Headed by Generals Pimentel and Benigno Filomeno de Rojas, it dispatched three commissioners to the capital to work out terms with La Gándara. When the shameful terms of this "Convention of Guibia" became known, Pimentel's government almost fell. Not only had the commissioners agreed to pay Spain an indemnity to cover all the expenses of the annexation (described as undertaken out of "motives of the highest generosity and nobility"); Spain was to be treated as a "most favored nation" and the Dominicans, with Spanish watchdogs at their side, were to guarantee no moves in the Caribbean prejudicial to Spain's interests.

Quickly repudiating his commissioners, Pimentel sent new envoys with instructions to offer no indemnities or binding treaties. La Gándara, unable to reverse the evacuation already ordered by Madrid, left a memento of Hispanic good will by destroying all the arms in sight, wrecking the public buildings, and taking women and children aboard as hostages for Spanish prisoners still in Dominican hands.

It would be pleasant to report that the Republic enjoyed peace and prosperity, emerging from the yoke of Spain, but the reverse is true. Santana was gone, but Baez came back—not once, but three times—in the decade of unlimited insurrections that was to follow the evacuation. With the principal cities devastated by warfare, the fields long uncultivated, the treasury empty, and the poverty of the masses abject, only a man with incontestible qualities of leadership could have restored order.

The country quickly became divided between two parties, and

neither party offered more than temporary relief from the other. Baez' faction, calling themselves "The Reds," was made up of the substantial merchants and small businessmen and found its principal support in the capital and along the south coast. Its only consistent "policy" was to print paper currency and endeavor to back this up with American dollars, paid in advance, first for the promised lease of Samaná as a naval base, and later for outright annexation of the country; and, failing in these, to accept a loan from a British banking house at ruinous rates of interest.

The "Blue" party, led by the planters and military leaders of the Cibao, fluctuated hopelessly between the liberal constitutionalism of such patriots as Ulises Espaillat and Arturo Meriño and the unprincipled rivalries of those soldiers who had managed to drive out the Spaniards but could never place the interests of the country as a whole above their personal jealousies. All of these soldiers became hopelessly dependent for sanctuary and arms on the two-faced friendship of Haiti. Only one of them, Gregorio Luperón, acted with any selflessness or consistency of purpose during this decade of constantly shifting fortunes. But it was Luperón's fatal weakness in refusing to accept power and exercise it himself for the general good that unwittingly prepared the way for the *coup d'état* of his own protégé, a man with none of Luperón's scruples and the first of the two absolute dictators who were to reap this whirlwind and govern with blood and iron for fifty years.

Baez' prestige in 1865 seems to have suffered not at all from the fact that he had flip-flopped into the Spanish camp the moment annexation became a certainty. If he was criticized for accepting a subsidy and the honorary rank of field marshal in the Spanish Army and for spending, as Welles put it, "the years during which his fellow-citizens were struggling for liberty in leading a life of luxurious ease in Europe," there is no record of it. With evacuation imminent, Baez resigned his field marshalship with a grand gesture and moved to Curaçao. On December 8, hailed by his own newspaper as "the angel of peace called to fulfill the patriotic mission of uniting the Dominicans and making them truly happy under the protection of a government which will guarantee all their rights," Baez was inaugurated president in Santo Domingo for the third time.

The inauspicious event was accompanied by two discordant notes. Padre Meriño, president of the national assembly, delivered a clear warning:

> Extraordinary things happen in this country. . . . Your star has once more risen upon the horizon of this Republic and you are called upon to occupy the Chief Magistracy. So unexpected an occurrence has prostrated with astonishment many who are now looking at you. . . . Speaking to you in the frank language of truth . . . I shall not avoid saying to you that you should labor under no illusions, since among a people like our own, to make use of the expression of an illustrious American orator, "It is as easy to pass from exile to supreme power as it is from supreme power to impeachment before the Bar of the Senate." . . . Sincere patriots, men of principle, all decent citizens, who desire, and are the only ones able, to give stability to the Government, are always disposed to support governments which are progressive and liberal, governments which are truly national. They only refuse their support and leave such governments at the mercy of their opponents, when they see them prostitute public interests to private interests, when they understand that despotism has banished justice from the seat of power, when, finally, they see in the stead of the Executive elected to labor for the happiness of the people, a sanguinary tyrant in the Presidential Chair, a perverse ruler or an audacious speculator who collects a colossal fortune, robbing the people of the riches which they have confided to him in order that he may procure peace, liberty and progress for his country. . . .

On the same day a revolution under Luperón, who was less disposed to wait and see whether Baez would repeat himself, broke out in Puerto Plata. Baez was strong enough to suppress that revolt, as well as subsequent ones inspired by Cabral and Pimentel, the Cibao leaders in his own cabinet, and he took the occasion, after jailing and executing those of his enemies he could seize, to abolish the liberal constitution of 1865 and govern henceforth by decree under the old constitution of 1854. This was provocation enough to make the Cibao rise again, and a fresh army of volunteers, led by Luperón and Pimentel, drove on the capital and forced Baez to flee to Curaçao.

On April 22, 1866, General Cabral was appointed provisional president as a compromise candidate, and on September 23 he was elected and inaugurated under the constitution of 1865. Cabral proved to be as susceptible to foreign blandishments as Baez, and even more inept. He failed to get his administration's agreement to the lease of Samaná.* When Baez' crony General Salnave replaced Haiti's President Geffrard, on whom Cabral had counted for policing of his western borders, Cabral's position was hopelessly exposed. On January 21, he and General Pimentel fled to Venezuela, and on May 2 Baez—who else—was inaugurated for the fourth time after modestly accepting the title "Great Citizen."

Without the slightest recognition of the irony of pursuing the very policy for which he had castigated Santana seven years before, Baez now reopened the negotiations to sell Samaná Peninsula to the United States. His opponents in the "Blue" party gave him little time. Cabral, Pimentel, and Luperón, using Haiti—where a revolt against the Baecista Salnave was already underway—as their base, began to move in on Baez from the southern and northern provinces. Stalled in his efforts to get financial help from the United States, Baez in his desperation negotiated a £757,700 loan in the spring of 1869 from a group of English bankers headed by Hartmont and Company.* With the bogus explanation that he wanted to build roads and railroads—Baez and his kind never build anything—the "Great Citizen" pledged the entire resources of the Republic to a bond issue, redeemable at par in cash after six months' notice, or at par by an accumulated sinking fund after twenty-five years by semiannual drawings. Luperón and his associates, meanwhile, having convinced the Haitian president that Baez' schemes for American annexation threatened the Negroes of both countries with slavery, concluded a mutual as-

* The full sequence of American efforts to take over the Dominican Republic, in part or in whole, will be given in chapter VIII.

* Later reduced to £420,000, with £100,000 going to Hartmont as a commission.

sistance treaty at St. Marc and renewed their offensive. Luperón's fears may have been exaggerated in this instance, but the presence of an American general at Samaná hoisting the stars and stripes in advance of Baez' latest effort to secure annexation could not be laughed off. There was nothing imaginary in the presence of an American fleet in Haitian and Dominican waters either. Baez made a frantic effort to rally popular support behind this impending grab by putting the question to a plebiscite, but the forced vote (16,000 to 11) fooled no one. When President Grant's attempt to secure annexation was defeated by the American Congress, Baez called for a second plebiscite to ratify the lease of Samaná Bay to a private American company for the ludicrous yearly rental of $150,000. The phony vote, this time 20,496 to 19, could not save Baez, who yielded to a revolution led by General Ignacio María González and fled the country on January 2, 1874.

González' government made a brave start. A general amnesty was declared. Luperón, Pimentel, and Cabral were invited back from exile. Freedom of press and of speech were guaranteed. Baez' Samaná Bay Company concession was canceled.

It was a comparatively mild uprising on the part of some of Baez' ousted bureaucrats that led González into the same trap that had closed over his predecessors. The false assumption that popular unrest can be dealt with only by abolishing freedom and restoring arbitrary executive powers had sunk the liberals of 1844 and 1863, and it promptly sank González. The proposition that the constitution must be violated to insure repression of dissent carried with it the corollary that a "backward" electorate could not be expected to pay its way in taxes and that only foreign loans could provide the wherewithal for—what? more effective repression?

A similar confusion, rising out of lack of fundamental principles or sense of direction, affected González' otherwise sound instinct for lasting friendship with Haiti. A treaty of peace, amity, commerce, navigation, and extradition signed on November 9, 1874, announced to the world that Hispaniola belonged to its inhabitants alone, and that neither country would permit the annexation or lease of any part of its territory to a foreign power. The existing boundary line, including territory seized by Haiti during the Boyer occupation, was recognized—generously, on the part of the Dominican Republic. And a project to build a railroad connecting the two capitals—as revolutionary in its implications as Caesar's welding of primitive Europe into Italy, or Peter the Great's incorporation of a western window in the medieval eastern facade of Russia—was agreed to by both nations. But González' foolish determination to get something for nothing, to momentarily replenish his empty coffers by painless means, insured the failure of the whole *rapprochement*. A clause of the treaty provided that in return for $150,000 to be paid to the Dominican treasury yearly for eight years, Haiti would enjoy free trade. Not only were the Dominican farmers in the west unable to compete with the low prices of the impoverished Haitian peasants; their farms were overrun by migrant cultivators and squatters.

The resulting economic ruin of the border provinces provided a perfect seedbed for the insurrectionary weed. Luperón, angered by the refusal of the González government to pay him $170,000 which he claimed as the losses incurred by him for six years of struggle against Baez, joined with other claimants of the Cibao in pressing for restitution. When Luperón's arrest was ordered, his lieutenant, Ulises Heureaux, and General Benito Monción seized Monte Cristi. Luperón himself captured Puerto Plata. When a working alliance between these "Blue" generals and the "Red" faction of Baez in the south was effected, González resigned.

No one really wanted Baez back, least of all Luperón. Once more there appeared to be a chance that a man of good will, selfless and farsighted, might emerge out of the stalemate of the carnivore. Such an idealist was Ulises Espaillat. On May 29, 1876, with Luperón's backing, he was elected president. It is noteworthy that this event preceded by just six weeks the death in Caracas of Juan Pablo Duarte, destitute and forgotten. More of an intellectual and less of a mystic than Duarte, Espaillat resembled the father of his country in being

utterly incorruptible and fearless. The keystone of his political philosophy—independence of all foreign entanglements—was also
Duarte's. It followed from this that Espaillat did not believe in mort-
gaging tomorrow to pay for today—" 'tomorrow,' " he declared,
"never dawns, and it is until tomorrow that we postpone our accomplishments." Stability must be paid for by taxation and, to be permanent, insured by education, freedom of speech and press, and an honest
judiciary. None of these measures, except perhaps the freedom to
provoke further insurrections, could be pleasing to the military
leaders who continued to dominate party politics. But with Luperón
as his war minister and a group of dedicated intellectuals as his other
cabinet members, it looked for a few weeks as if the new president
might accomplish something.

Espaillat's enemies, unfortunately, gave him no time even to try
out his reforms. Within eight weeks of his inauguration two insurrections had assumed formidable proportions. In the southwest, long a
stronghold of the Baecistas, a band of malcontents declared their
independence. An insurrection in the north, under González' partisans, was put down by Luperón's chief of staff, General Heureaux;
but with help from the new ruler of Haiti, a friend of Baez, the
rebels managed by midsummer to control most of the Cibao. As early
as July, Espaillat, beginning to be deserted by even his close friends,
expressed his discouragement in a moving letter to General Cabral:

> You already know, doubtless, that what was in the beginning the
> insignificant foray of a small gang has today assumed the proportions of
> a formal insurrection which the legitimate authorities of the Cibao are
> struggling with all their power to suppress.
>
> That means that I, who made the immense sacrifice of accepting the
> Presidency because of the compelling argument that my acceptance of the
> office was absolutely essential if public order was to be preserved, have
> now to consent that the force of arms, civil war, be the means of main-
> taining me in power: power of which I never was enamored and which
> I am exercising with profound distaste.
>
> And if in offering my name, until now respected as that of a man of
> worth, lacking unworthy ambition, as that of an honored patriot—if in

offering this name, which is the sole legacy which I desire to bequeath to my children, as a sacrifice upon the altar of the duty of a public man, I could have the assurance that I was doing it as a tribute to that portion of the Dominican people who still have some esteem for honor and the dictates of "men of order," I would make the sacrifice in all resignation; but when there is not a day that passes since I assumed the fatal presidency which does not bring with it a bitter disillusion from those from whom I least expected it; when I see that instead of comprehension of my situation and instead of loyal and vigorous assistance I encounter only unjustifiable demands, unfounded discontent, indifference and aversion on the part of the men whom I truly esteem and upon whose cooperation I most counted . . . then, my dear General, a feeling of absolute despair gains possession of my soul. What, after all, can I think of such insanity?

Two months ago the presence of these men in the north, once Gabino (Crespo) was defeated by General Heureaux, made triumph sure, and would have calmed all passions, implanting confidence in our friends and respect among our enemies. Today, it is necessary to ruin the Republic, calling upon the south to rise against these egotistical and factious rebels. What an aftermath of deplorable consequences can one foresee!

I do not know what excuse they can offer to public opinion, to God, to their own conscience, those very men who not three months ago raised me to the Presidency; and I without giving them the least motive, without changing in the slightest degree either my program of administration or my principles, both of which were fully known beforehand; today it seems as if they took pleasure in discrediting me and in bringing about my downfall, as if they had solely wished to elevate me in order to obtain the satisfaction of casting me down. . . .

The note of self-pity in this cry of anguish does not make it less truthful as a memorial to the death of Dominican liberalism. Espaillat made a last despairing public appeal for support in September, but on October 5 the capital was seized by a group of González' supporters, and on December 20 the great liberal retired to his home in Santiago. "González and his gang," wrote Luperón of the successor whose presidency lasted just forty days, "were no more than the spider which ensnared Espaillat . . . behind them came Baez, who was the cat." In the sense that a cat is supposed to have nine lives, the simile was apt, but Baez' fifth presidency was to be his shortest and his last. González had fled to Port-au-Prince where he persuaded Haiti's president that a revolution against Baez would be to their mutual advantage. The border provinces sprang to arms, and a few months later, aroused by Padre Meriño, the eastern provinces followed suit. When Baez' principal defending force was cut to pieces by General Cesareo Guillermo's volunteer Seyban army, the "Great Citizen" made his final exit, this time to Puerto Rico. But not before he had forced the local merchants to pay him $70,000 in advance of customs fees and deposited abroad an additional $300,000, accumulated by withholding the salaries of the civil servants he had asked to remain in office and the soldiers who were defending him in the field.

Ulises Espaillat, disillusioned and broken-hearted, died on April 25, 1878. Had he lived just one more week, he would have had the satisfaction of seeing the departure from the scene of the man who had done more than any Dominican to make his country weak, disrespected, and ungovernable. Had he been able to envision the aftermath, however, the price to be paid for replacing immoral weakness with immoral strength, Espaillat might have counted himself blessed to close his eyes when he did.

VII

Partial Eclipse, 1879-99

The Second Failure of Liberalism and the Dictatorship of Ulises Heureaux

Ulises Heureaux, the Negro general who ruled the Dominican Republic mercilessly for most of the two last decades of the century, differed from the dictators who preceded him in several important respects. Reckless courage, an heroic physique, military genius, and a charismatic attraction for the illiterate masses were positive qualities he shared with Pedro Santana. The entirely negative capabilities of Buenaventura Baez—to maintain oneself in power by filling offices with fawning parasites, to float loans among the competitive powers by dangling territorial bribes in front of them, and when all else failed, to print paper money—were Heureaux's too. But there the similarities cease.

"Lilís"—the childhood nickname by which Heureaux was popularly known throughout his career—was a modern autocrat in more ways than one. Neither glory nor money were his major motivations. Power, to have and to hold, was his lifelong preoccupation. For the first thirty-seven years of Heureaux's life, he schooled himself in the means of seizing power in such a way that, once entrenched, he would have no serious rivals. During his last seventeen years, he directed all

of his volcanic energy and talents to creating such an ambience of
servile dependence and fear that no one dared challenge him. Only
by looking ahead to the equally ruthless and "successful" career of
Rafael Leonidas Trujillo Molina in our time, can any accurate com-
parisons be found for the method and madness of Ulises Heureaux.

Like Trujillo, Heureaux began his long reign by buying up such
of his military rivals as were for sale and subjecting the rest to vilifi-
cation, exile, or murder. Like Trujillo, he employed an army of spies,
sending them as far afield in search of conspiracies as Paris and
New York, and not hesitating (in the case of a writer who had published articles against him in Puerto Rico) to send assassins in pursuit abroad. Like Trujillo, who treated his private accounts and those
of the government as identical, Heureaux was a builder. Unlike his
predecessors, he left the country richer in industries, agriculture, and
communications—and his friends and relatives richer in the process.
Even in respect to having no personal vices except blood lust and an
insatiable, promiscuous sexuality, the parallel holds. Heureaux had
procurers everywhere, and one isolated town boasted uniqueness for
not harboring one of his mistresses. Only in respect to the techniques
of the modern totalitarian state, still to be invented by Hitler and
Stalin—the single party, the mass rallies, the propaganda mills, the
rewriting of history, the indoctrination of children, the racial perse-
cution, the military juggernaut—did Ulises Heureaux yield anything
in refinements of despotism to his infamous successor.

The anecdotes of Heureaux that survive are revealing. While minister of interior under Meriño, he heard that his own brother-in-law
was implicated in a plot. Inviting him to dinner, he asked him
whether he had enjoyed the meal, and upon receiving an enthusiastic
response, said: "I am glad of that, for I am about to have you shot.
Have a cigar. It will be your last." On another occasion Heureaux
took a dinner guest, a general, for a stroll, and when his guest asked
why some men were digging an odd-shaped trench by the roadside,
Heureaux replied: "They are digging your grave"; before his friend
could recover from his consternation, a squad of soldiers appeared

and executed him where he stood. Heureaux's humor was not always so deadly. Once when a French admiral arrived at Santo Domingo with two warships to enforce a claim to some funds the dictator had no intention of relinquishing, he turned to the Frenchman and asked, "Admiral, are you familiar with the Darwin theory?" Surprised, the visitor asked what he was driving at. Heureaux apologized for the way in which he had phrased the question. "I myself believe in it thoroughly. I am convinced that the Negro is a descendent of the monkeys, and you know, Admiral, once a monkey gets his hands upon something he never lets go." Heureaux's French was said to be good, but his English, judging by this account by an American who had asked him if he intended to kill the latest of his enemies, had a British West Indian twang: "What good it do me if I kill he? Then he brother, he father, he wife—all make my enemy. But if I put he in preeson, and then take he out, and feed he, and give he clothe, he's family all my frien'."

Unfortunately, not many of Ulises Heureaux's enemies were treated with such kindness, except perhaps in the early days of his rule. He had learned in fifteen years of military campaigning against a constantly disappearing and recurring opposition that only a dead enemy never returns. Heureaux stated once that he was not concerned with what history might say about him since he would not be there to read it. Possibly because he had no Dominican blood in his veins, he had more contempt than pity for a people who could be misled so easily. "The black man can only be ruled by fear," he told an American correspondent, "and the half-breed is even more treacherous."

He was born in Puerto Plata on October 21, 1845, the illegitimate son of a Haitian, d'Assas Heureaux, by a Negress of St. Thomas named Josefa Lebel. It was the year following liberation from Boyer's twenty-year occupation, and the racial lines separating the two countries had become almost indistinguishable. To call Heureaux a Haitian as Sumner Welles does, and to add that, "as is psychologically so often the case in those of Heureaux's race," responsibility becomes so unbearable that "the mental functions . . . finally break down," is to feed on fantasy—and to miss the point. In the context of Dominican politics, Heureaux did no more than bring the consequences of rule by unprincipled adventurers one step closer to the absolute. Compared with many Caucasian military men engaged in politics— General Grant, Marshal Pétain, Colonel Perón, to mention three— Heureaux conducted the state's affairs with remarkable aplomb.

Schooled in Puerto Plata by an English Methodist missionary, and apprenticed briefly in the store of a French merchant, the young Heureaux decided that even begging in the streets was preferable to piety or salesmanship. Growing up, he joined the bands of young desperadoes along the Haitian border. Six feet, four inches tall, handsome, valorous, and a born leader, Heureaux found soldiering to his taste. Attracting the attention of Luperón during the wars of the restoration, he rose rapidly to become chief of staff to that patriot commander. Although a large part of Luperón's autobiography, written years later while he was in exile from his protégé's dictatorship, is devoted to portraying in Heureaux the evolution of "a barbaric savage . . . a thousand times worse than Santana and Baez," the General freely admits that Heureaux "never in any conflict showed the least discouragement," was "unfailingly fearless, resolute and resourceful," and became the officer in whom his chief "placed most confidence." But in attempting to explain how the "military genius" became the "infamous politician," Luperón offers no insight. "As the son of a Yankee [*sic*] and a Haitian woman," he lamely says, "Heureaux inherited all that is worst in both races."

The two weak and corrupt regimes that succeeded the final exodus of Baez in 1878—those headed by Ignacio María González and by Cesareo Guillermo—were overthrown by Luperón with the assistance of Heureaux. As provisional president in the last month of 1879, one of Luperón's first acts was to delegate authority in the capital to his brilliant lieutenant. Remaining in the Cibao himself, he refused to accept the constitutional presidency. In the year that passed before the election of Archbishop Meriño as president (September 1, 1880), Luperón carried out notable reforms. But most of them, ironically, together with those undertaken by Meriño himself, only served to prepare the way effectively for the impending dictatorship of Heureaux. Luperón passed a conscription law, reorganized the national army, replenished the arsenal with modern weapons, paid the salaries of the bureaucracy ($200,000 in arrears), adjusted foreign claims, and refused to accept any more "bribes" from Haiti under the González treaty of 1874. Archbishop Meriño, firmly backed by his old friend Luperón, brought about an unprecedented prosperity. He encouraged immigration from Cuba and Puerto Rico. He commenced the planting of the great sugar estates along the south coast. But in using his minister of the interior, Ulises Heureaux, as the instrument to suppress two minor rebellions, the iron-willed archbishop did not hesitate to execute his enemies, including even the wounded and boys of fifteen, when they were found bearing arms. He also abolished the right of asylum in foreign consulates. When the honest but intolerant priest's term of office expired in the summer of 1882, it was a foregone conclusion that he and Luperón would give their blessings to General Heureaux's candidacy. It was just as self-evident that with their backing Lilís would be elected by an overwhelming majority.

The two years of Heureaux's first term were deceptively wholesome. Freedom of speech and of the press continued to be respected. The usual sporadic rebellions in the Cibao were stamped out with Heureaux's customary vigor. A secret donation of $50,000 from President Salamon, Haiti's dictator, who wished to see his friend prosper, was gratefully received. Prosperity continued, with a record governmental annual income of $3,000,000; and if, after no more than $800,000 of it had been dispersed, there still remained a total deficit of $300,000, certainly the minister of hacienda, General Marchena, who was declared by Heureaux to be a financial wizard, could not be charged with the discrepancy. After all, as Luperón put it,

> There exists in the Dominican Republic the mistaken theory that any man who can figure must be an economist, and it is for that reason that

almost always, through some fatality, Governments appoint a Minister of Hacienda who has failed in his own business and who fails consequently to a greater degree in the business of the State.

Not feeling strong enough yet to perpetuate himself in office by altering the constitution, Heureaux set about undermining those leaders of the "Blue" party who were most likely to become strong candidates themselves. Luperón, above all, must be cut down. Lilís began by calling a conference of the country's top leaders to agree upon a single ticket, and after privately assuring each one of the aspirants that his candidacy would receive presidential support, grimly watched the resulting failure to agree upon anyone. When the field had finally narrowed down to three aspirant—Vice President de Moya, General Billini, and General Imbert—Heureaux looked on with satisfaction as Meriño supported Billini and Luperón came out for Imbert. Then, when de Moya withdrew and agreed to run for vice president on Imbert's ticket, Heureaux "reluctantly" announced his own support of General Billini.

The election was rigged from the start, but even while he was having the ballot boxes in the capital stuffed to insure Billini's election, Heureaux wrote Luperón a hypocritical letter, signed "Your affectionate son," promising to support Imbert should he triumph. So sure of Imbert's victory were his followers in the Cibao that they were celebrating victory even as the news arrived that Billini had been elected by the narrow margin of two thousand votes.

With passions out of control and the "Blue" party now divided for the first time in twenty years, it remained for the crafty ex-President to dispose of his well meaning but stubborn successor. This he accomplished by spreading the rumor that General Cesareo Guillermo —who had returned to the country under an amnesty proclaimed by Billini—had come to plot, with Billini's aid, the demise of Luperón. The congress withdrew its support of Billini, and when an insurrection seemed imminent, the peace loving President resigned and was succeeded by the vice president, General Woss y Gil, who promptly appointed a cabinet of Heureaux's partisans and dispatched the latter on a well publicized naval expedition to hunt down General Guillermo in Azua. Grateful to Heureaux for having brought about the death of his old enemy Guillermo, Luperón now fell into Lilís' trap once and for all. Not only did he come out in support of Heureaux in the presidential elections of 1886; he persuaded General Segundo Imbert to run for vice president on the same ticket. When Heureaux's opponents, de Moya and Billini, refused to accept the verdict of another fraudulent election and called for a revolution in the Cibao, Heureaux, with Luperón's tacit support, was able to drive them, together with Benito Monción, last of the old restoration "Blues," across the border into Haiti.

"Blues" or "Reds," it mattered not to Heureaux; installed for life now, he gathered them all into his fold. Loyalty to his person became the sole criterion for advancement, and indeed for survival. And again foreshadowing Trujillo, "as soon as the Dictator learned that any member of the younger generation showed exceptional talent or gave promise of becoming a man of prominence, an agent of the President invariably approached him to attempt to secure his support for the Dictator." To be sure that he would be there to profit by their support, the President now proceeded to revise the constitution, lengthening the term of office and abolishing direct elections; an electoral college could be more easily counted on to make the right choices.

> There is no more interesting chapter in the modern history of the Americas [wrote Welles] than that which contains the account of the manner in which the Dictator of a small country, with but small resources and of but potential importance, played off, one against the other, the United States of America and the great European Powers.

The American consul to Santo Domingo, appointed by President Hayes (and later to be dismissed by President Cleveland for larceny and the "indecent proposal" that Columbus' bones be exhibited in American circus side shows), became the first of the hypnotic Heureaux's enthusiastic confidants. The Dictator began by dropping hints: whereas Luperón favored the lease of Samaná to a French

syndicate, he, Heureaux, would be happy to revive the defunct
Samaná Bay Company and do business with it. Prolonged efforts to
work out a reciprocal trade treaty having come to nothing, Heureaux
resorted with more success to attracting American business enterprises. Unfortunately for both countries, however, most of these
concessionaires were, in the words of an American consul, "adventurers who are dissipated, dishonest and immoral." One such, a
gentleman from Texas who had read in the New York *Sun* that
General Heureaux was inviting Negro Americans to settle in the
Dominican Republic, wrote the Consul to say that immigration from
Texas would be

> . . . a grand success. There are fully 5,000 well-to-do farmers in this
> section who would willingly emigrate to San Domingo if they knew the
> true condition of the country. I have suggested to the President that an
> agent should be employed. . . . I am selling a life-size picture of Toussant
> L'Ouverture [*sic*], which sells at sight here. Do you think it would sell
> well in San Domingo? I also have the noted silver plater [*sic*]. Do you
> think I could do much in the Island with it? . . .
>
> (Sgd)————
> San Marcos, Texas.
>
> P.S.—The Separate Coach Bill has passed and I am anxious to get out of
> Texas.

In Heureaux's second administration, as the government's expenses rose in reflection of the President's increasingly lavish establishment and sartorial vanity, the search for new sources of income
became feverish. Payment of salaries in the various departments once
again lagged by a year or more. To their usual claims for "just compensation," the ex-revolutionaries appended veiled threats. A proposal to lease Samaná Bay with all its keys to President Cleveland
for a $4,000,000 loan had met with stony silence. A group of New
York capitalists, though tempted by the unprecedented offer that they
collect 30 per cent of all Dominican revenues themselves to cover
interest and amortization charges, refused to advance $1,350,000 in
gold. General Marchena's effort to obtain funds in Europe was
seized upon by the British, still fuming over Dominican default on

the Hartmont loan of 1869, to demand that its bondholders be compensated in advance of any other financial deals. Since a British company was now engaged in constructing a railway between Santiago and Samaná, blackmail was in order.

The impasse was finally overcome for Heureaux when Marchena negotiated a contract with Westendorp and Company of Amsterdam. Under its terms the Dominican government was to authorize the creation of £770,000 thirty-year 6 per cent gold bonds. Of this sum, £142,860 was to be employed in the conversion of the outstanding bonds of the Hartmont loan at the rate of one to five, £151,660 was to be expended in the payment of the interior floating indebtedness, while the remainder was to be bought by Westendorp at 78 per cent of the bonds' nominal value.

This financial "shot in the arm," which accomplished nothing for the average Dominican except to perpetuate for another ten years the dictatorship under which he was groveling, was paid for by an arrangement carrying fatal consequences to the nation's sovereignty. Westendorp refused even to consider the contract unless the interest and amortization charges should become a first lien on the Republic's customs revenues. Westendorp further insisted that its own agents (called a *régie*) be empowered to collect *all* customs duties, turning over to the government the remainder in a humiliating monthly dole of $75,000. The alien moneylenders even had the gall to demand that if yearly customs revenues should *exceed* a certain figure, its own commission and expense accounts must be increased! The congress, with its salaries at stake, was forced to ratify the contract. By thus infringing the nation's sovereignty, the process was set in motion by which, ultimately, the United States—to satisfy its own claims—would move from the customs house to the national palace.

In the same autumn month of 1888, General Luperón, still under the illusion that he could match wits with his protégé in the political arena, and showing the same naïveté in trusting Lilís' word that he had shown two years before, resolved to run against Heureaux for the presidency. He was reassured by a joint manifesto Heureaux induced him to sign proclaiming that no coercion or fraud would be employed and that each candidate would respect the other. It was to be the aging patriot's last move on the political chessboard. His aides were promptly thrown into jail by Heureaux for "disturbing the peace," and Luperón himself withdrew from the race, leveling bitter charges against his former chief of staff and ultimately going into exile in Puerto Rico where he would write his acrimonious memoires.

Ruling through a dummy, Don Manuel María Gautier, who slyly appointed Luperón's old comrades in the "Blue" party to his principal cabinet posts, Heureaux—obsessed as always to outmaneuver the Republic's friends and enemies abroad—now turned his attention to Haiti. Supporting General Hippolite in a successful struggle to overthrow President Légitime (whose name was no help to him), Heureaux received in return the ouster from Haitian soil of his old enemy General de Moya, at the same time insuring—as he had in the past—that Haiti would be governed by a ruler willing to police the border and to provide financial assistance should a new crisis require it.

With consummate skill the Dictator now played off the mounting protests of the German, French, and British governments—over violations of most-favored-nation clauses in their treaties—against the United States, which was actually getting the favors and which Heureaux induced from time to time to make known its "moral support." The German government, on which the planters of the Cibao depended for Germany's virtually exclusive purchase of the tobacco crop, posed the greatest potential threat, but was forced by American pressure to back down. Using the perpetual negotiations with Washington for Samaná as a lever, Heureaux now tried to get a second loan from Westendorp. But that company, inquiring into the drying up of the customs revenues earmarked to pay the interest on its first loan and discovering that the Dictator had been privately accepting cash advances from local importers which exempted them from paying duties, flatly refused. Heureaux now turned to a New

York syndicate, later to be euphemistically known as the San Domingo Improvement Company. This Wall Street group, for a further and self-perpetuating strangle hold on the Republic's resources, not only took over from Westendorp, but gave Heureaux everything he wanted in the form of two new loans totaling $11,000,000. It mattered not at all to Lilís that the Dominican government was now receiving only a pittance of $90,000 a month in silver from the occupied customs and that the *régie* was set to ride the overburdened back of the Republic for decades to come.

As the presidential election of 1893 drew near, it became clear that the Dictator's financial medicine man, General Marchena, who had indeed been responsible for securing the European loans, would wish to run against the President himself. He should have known better. Not only was it assured that he would lose the election; since he had the temerity to propose a change from American to French protection, with a proviso that the purse strings be transferred from the chief executive to the congress, it was more than probable that he would lose his life as well. He did, in fact, lose both: the first with dispatch, the second after excruciating torment.

With Marchena out of the way and a last Luperón-inspired putsch from Haiti crushed at Monte Cristi, it might be thought that Heureaux could now have partially relaxed the iron grip in which he held every public and private institution in the country. On the contrary, following the inexorable law of personal despotisms, the last seven years of Heureaux's rule became a reign of terror. Like Trujillo in his later years, Heureaux trusted no one; furthermore, he became financially more and more dependent on outside aid as the army of spies and informers ate up the meager funds allotted to him by his customs overseers. Like Trujillo, too, he became a miser, guarding his private fortune and living in mounting fear of assassination. As early as 1893 he had written the American consul:

My city properties located in this City have a total value of about $200,000 in gold. Knowing, as I do, things in my country, and having to foresee the dangers which may affect my own person and perhaps my interests as well, I should be glad to place the latter under the protection of the American nation, leaving to your judgement the manner and the form in which that desire may be realized. . . .

Terror was no longer concealed. The presidential gunboat, on periodic circuits of the coast line, returned to the capital with cargoes of suspects. So overcrowded did the fortress prison become that Heureaux gave orders that its surplus population be thrown to the sharks at the base of the cliff, along with the garbage. The mistresses Heureaux maintained in every settlement throughout the country provided him with information on the daily lives and even thoughts of the humblest of his subjects; and his secret agents in Haiti, Venezuela, Puerto Rico, New York, Paris, London, and Berlin supplemented this monumental dossier with reports on every movement of the growing regiment of his enemies abroad.

It was not enough. Horacio Vásquez, one of the idealistic young generals who had participated in Luperón's last sortie, now organized in Puerto Rico the first counterpart of Duarte's "Trinitarios," an association of young patriots calling themselves "Junta Revolucionaria de Jóvenes." Heureaux had been attracted some years before by the young Vásquez' conspicuous talents and bearing, but one day in Moca, hearing the Dictator give an order—"Wherever you go, your soldiers are to consider as their property all horses, cows, chickens—and women"—the young colonel had resigned in disgust, been imprisoned, escaped, been hunted across the country, and forced to flee into the exile where he joined Luperón and other refugees. The junta finally dissolved, but its ablest young leaders—Vásquez, Federico Velásquez, and Ramón Cáceres—reunited in Moca, where, pretending to renounce politics for the care of their neglected plantations, they were permitted to plot the tyrant's downfall.

Vásquez at this point made a mistake that was to plague him—and his country—for the next twenty-five years. Instead of reconstituting his youth movement and entrusting the Republic's future to men whose interests were not deeply involved with property and privilege, Vásquez offered the leadership to Juan Isidro Jiménez, the nation's wealthiest planter and a man totally lacking in character or vision. Vásquez should have been forewarned; back in the days of the exiled "Junta" he had tendered its command to Jiménez, then in Paris, only to have the vain merchant decline and publish the telegram, thus throwing into Heureaux's clutches some of the latter's principal enemies. In June of 1898 Jiménez had essayed a lunatic coup of his own, buying an American ship and sailing it to Monte Cristi with an immense cargo of arms. Heureaux was waiting, and from the resulting fiasco only the selfish Jiménez, with money to bribe his passage to the Bahamas, escaped. Yet once the Dictator had been assassinated (with no help from Jiménez), he was the man who Vásquez was to foist upon the liberated country as the "Supreme Chief of the Revolution." Once again that fatal unwillingness to assume personal responsibility which had paralyzed Dominican liberalism from Duarte to Luperón, was manifested in Horacio Vásquez' curious miscalculation.

The blazing act of tyrannicide had taken place without Vásquez' direct support, although it had his blessing. Vásquez was still arguing for an old-style insurrection when Ramón Cáceres, a more astute and impulsive young man who had been brought up to believe that Heureaux had murdered his father, talked the conspirators into letting him try to exterminate the tyrant himself. Accompanied only by Jacobito Lara, a boy of sixteen, and deserted by the others who had agreed to face the Dictator with them as he passed through the main street of Moca on his way to Santiago, Cáceres stepped boldly up to Heureaux and fired several shots into him. Symbolically, Lilís' only answering shot went wild, killing a beggar on the outskirts of the crowd; he had fired involuntarily with his right hand, mutilated years before when he himself had been a beggar, in a struggle for possession of a blanket. Before a single member of the bodyguard could recover from stupefaction, Cáceres and his companion passed through their midst unscathed, mounted horse, and joined

Vásquez and the main body of conspirators outside the town. That night all of them rode into Moca and proclaimed the revolution of July 26, 1899.

Thus ended Ulises Heureaux, even in the manner of his death a harbinger of things to come. He who had started with such promise, a hero of the liberation of his country from Spain; he who had inherited in his initial presidency the first genuine peace and prosperity since the early days of the colony; he who was probably the last man who could have united all Hispaniola—had thus been promisingly described by the American chargé d'affaires in 1890:

> It was pleasant to see a man in his position attending to the carting of his own luggage instead of leaving it to others, as he might have done without touching it with one of his fingers. . . . He is a tall, slender, bright-eyed man of dark complexion and well-defined negroid features. He gave me his age as forty-two, but he looks even younger than that. He is of wiry make-up and has apparently a large capacity for work. Beside his native language he speaks French and English, the latter remarkably well. He is a man of energy and intelligence and his history proves him to be well-versed in statesmanship.

Seven years later, without reference to the price paid in blood and loss of sovereignty, the aging autocrat proudly listed the balance sheet of his accomplishments—railroads, submarine cables, telegraph lines, public buildings, wharves and docks, the foundations of monopolistic agriculture and industry, an efficient army and navy, newspapers, schools, and local bureaus wherewith to tighten the central government's authority. Sumner Welles, with no thought of the deadly second round ahead, toted up, as if clairvoyantly, the debit side of Lilís' ledger:

> The substitution of corruption for integrity as the norm in administration; the suffocation of that impulse towards liberal government by Constitutional methods which had brought Gonzalez first to the Presidency, and which had later showed signs of growth under Espaillat; the immense increase in the public debt by loans of which not one penny had been

expended for the public profit; the stifling of all national agriculture and industry development except that promoted by foreign capital; the centralization of the opportunities for commercial expansion among the favoured few; the imprisonment, execution or assassination of numberless victims; the impairment of the nation's sovereignty and the barter of its territory; the disintegration of political parties through the corruption or removal of the leaders of public thought among the educated classes; and, above all, the consistent effort to obliterate those ideals of liberty and patriotism, maintained by the founders of the Republic, from the hearts of that younger generation upon which the hope of the salvation of the Republic rested.

VIII

The American Occupation, 1900-24

Before, During, and After the Landing of the Marine Corps

If there is such a thing as poetic justice, it may be said to operate blindly, bringing about the succession of evil by good in accordance with the revulsion unmitigated evil inspires; but it carries no moral imperatives of its own. A good man, once projected into power by a fateful act of violence, however necessary, must prove himself; and the act of violence, unless it be exorcized by an assumption of the common guilt and vigilance against lawlessness itself, can be reinvoked by the very evil it was originally designed to destroy.

Ramón Cáceres was a good man, and his presidency (1906-11) was the freest, most peaceful, most genuinely constructive in his country's history. He was also a big man—warm-hearted, amply proportioned, generous, jovial, and brave to the point of foolhardiness. His ruddy complexion and sanguine temperament come through the posed, official portrait—ribbons of honor, Edwardian moustaches, and all. Heureaux's eyes bulge with an excess of lust and egotism; they are penetrating but nonreceptive. Vásquez' eyes are set too close together; he has a look of being aware of his own virtue. Cáceres' eyes are very far apart. There is nothing excessive in any of his features; Hispanic pride mellowed by a touch of the Negro; a noble Dominican face. Cáceres was a practical politician, in the best American sense of that phrase, recognizing his own limitations, appointing able men to deal with technical questions beyond his competence. His obvious honesty brought him men's trust. His simplicity and openheartedness made him loved.

Cáceres had not come to power easily. The chaos following Heureaux's assassination was compounded by the ambitions of his many would-be successors. Horacio Vásquez, Cáceres' friend and elder cousin as well as his nominal chief, became provisional president on August 29, 1899. After taking some completely necessary steps to redeem the paper currency with which the country was deluged, Vásquez announced that he would support Juan Isidro Jiménez in the forthcoming election. Why the popular idol Vásquez felt called upon to make this self-effacing gesture in unclear. Perhaps he thought such a gesture was the only possible one that could set a public example of patriotism.

The mistaken belief was widespread that Jiménez, reputedly a millionaire, would share his fortune with the people. But the phrase "Jiménez viene con dinero," a local wit said, could better have been rendered "Jiménez viene *por* dinero," for apart from the burning desire to recoup his fortune, Jiménez seems to have had no guiding purpose whatsoever. Appointing Vásquez and Cáceres to relatively minor posts in the provinces, the new President quickly became embroiled with the French. After permitting himself to be bailed out of this threatening situation by the Americans, Jiménez ran head on into the popular hostility to Uncle Sam, an inevitable heritage of Heureaux's flirtation with the San Domingo Improvement Company and other shabby Wall Street operations.

Spontaneous uprisings against Jiménez in the Cibao were kept under control by Vásquez until he discovered that his mercenary protégé had reopened his private export-import house in Monte Cristi and was profiting from it under governmental aegis—at competitors' expense. Censured by congress for improper financial practices, Jiménez attempted to divert attention by mounting a punitive expedition against Vice President Vásquez. This was too much. Vásquez finally joined the rebels. The revolution proclaimed on April 26, 1902, spread like brushfire. Supported by no one, Jiménez capitulated. In a matter of days Vásquez entered the capital at the head of his troops and treated his countrymen to the unprecedented spectacle of a victor who took no vengeance and who indeed protected the members of the outgoing administration until they could go their various ways in peace.

Once more, Provisional President Vásquez embarked manfully upon a program of reform. He established a national bureau of education to put into effect the pedagogical reforms advocated by Eugenio de Hostos, a visionary Puerto Rican educator. He prohibited the private importation of arms. He encouraged large-scale agriculture. An attempt was even made to bring the government's revenues and expenditures into balance.

None of these measures—nor the bottomless reserve of good will that even his enemies acknowledged—were enough to save Vásquez from the political ineptitude that dogged his career. At once ambitious and selfless, sometimes too humble and sometimes too righteous, Vásquez constantly wavered between a policy of *laissez faire* when local outbreaks threatened the peace and a noble, Luperón-like withdrawal from the arena when crises multiplied.

It is impossible to find any connecting links, save this constitutional vacillation, in the chain of events that finally led to the capture of the capital by the Jimenista General Woss y Gil in the summer of 1903 and the flight of both Vásquez and Cáceres to Cuba. Among the contributory factors were: Vásquez' refusal to continue the subsidies with which Jiménez had bribed the local *caciques;* a temporary falling out between Vásquez and Cáceres over who should run for vice president in the next constitutional election (both finally agreed to support a weaker compromise candidate); the advantage taken of the liberals' amnesty to Heureaux's old camp followers; the chronic political chaos in Haiti, which continued to provide bases for dissident insurrectionaries; and finally the financial incapacity of the federal government to cope with the mounting costs of suppressing local outbreaks.

Woss y Gil's government, which lasted barely four months, accomplished nothing except to increase the indebtedness of the Republic by another $700,000. It also brought foreign intervention one step closer. Marines were now being landed periodically from warships to "protect" their "nationals." And proposals to seize the customhouses outright were gaining support in various foreign capitals. Receiving little support from Jiménez, who rankled at not being called upon to head the government himself, Woss y Gil was forced to make alliances with those Horacistas still in the country. General Cáceres, who had now returned from Cuba, put an end to this tactic on the part of Vásquez' old followers. General Carlos Morales declared the inevitable revolution on October 23, and although it seemed for a while, as Welles put it, "as if the Jimenistas and Horacistas participating in this revolution might postpone their attempt to overthrow the Government until they had annihilated one another," the Jimenista general entered the capital on November 24.

So sure was Jiménez, ever watchful, that this constituted his cue to reassume the presidential mantle, that he left New York as soon as Morales' proclamation was made. Unfortunately for him, he had reckoned without the ambitions of the erratic Morales, who saw at once that with Horacista support (what wouldn't they do to keep Jiménez out!), he could usurp the leadership for himself. Barely had Morales announced his candidacy, and the news that General Cáceres would be his running mate, when a new revolution broke out. It failed—in part because Morales, with federal gunboats in his possession, was able to move his troops from port to port with more speed than Jiménez; in part because Cáceres at last succeeded, by means of a published letter, in arousing the public to a recognition of Jiménez' motives.

Morales and Cáceres were inaugurated president and vice president on June 19, 1904, their cabinet being divided between Horacistas and those Jimenistas who had abandoned Jiménez. But the opposition party, headed by Jiménez himself, began to recoup some of its lost popularity by denouncing Morales' increasing dependence on United States support. Not only did Morales make American operation of the customhouses the primary aim of his foreign policy; he attempted to negotiate a treaty under which the Republic would be placed under direct American protection for fifty years. Jiménez' followers, naturally enough, were not impressed by the plausible argument that control of the customs by native political parties only guaranteed that the nation's resources would constantly be used to foment or suppress revolutions. Nor was their anti-American propaganda weakened when a company of Marines landed near the capital and temporarily seized Villa Duarte in reprisal for the shooting (by Jimenistas) of the pilot of one of the U.S.S. *Yankee*'s launches.

Jiménez' effort to counter the government's pro-Americanism by enlisting the support of Germany and Haiti, however, did nothing to enhance the aura of "patriotism" in which that adventurer sought to wrap his cause. In foreign affairs, as we shall see when summarizing briefly the succession of events that led up to the United States receivership of 1905, Morales succeeded well. In domestic affairs he failed dismally. Forced more and more into the background by the Horacistas in his cabinet, and specifically eclipsed by the growing popularity of Vice President Cáceres, Morales turned for personal salvation to his old friends, the Jimenistas. Sneaking out of the capital on Christmas Night of 1905, the President joined a band of conspirators and proceeded to launch a revolution against his own government! Receiving no popular support and having broken his leg while being dragged from one place of concealment to another, he finally addressed a pathetic request for asylum to the American minister. Carried through the streets on a litter under the eyes of a great crowd assembled to savor his humiliation, he was placed aboard an American warship and taken to Puerto Rico. Returning now from Cuba, General Vásquez, though in poor health, led a campaign which scattered the remaining Jimenistas. Refusing the presidency, he threw his support to his old friend, the Vice President; and on February 20, 1906, Ramón Cáceres assumed the office that he was to occupy so ably for the next five years.

If any rational cause can be given for the tragic undoing of President Cáceras in 1911, it must be the unnatural relationship then existing between the Dominican Republic and the United States. The Dominican Republic had everything to gain and nothing to lose by cooperating with the enlightened policy of President Theodore Roosevelt and his secretary of state, Elihu Root, in 1906. Yet so basically unsound and humiliating was the historical foundation of this relationship that no Dominican government, however rational its immediate economic motives might be, could hope to overcome completely the moral-political consequences of such a policy.

Cáceres' minister of hacienda, Federico Velásquez, was a brilliant intellectual who recognized that the prosperity of his country and the stability of his chief's government were wholly dependent upon cooperation with the policy of the Roosevelt administration. And yet it was precisely because Velásquez bore the brunt of the unpopularity which this policy engendered among those who could not understand it, making no attempt to mollify the suspicion and hatred of a great power, that Cáceres was able to retain his own popularity and survive for so long the various nationalistic attempts to overthrow him.

While the prosperity following the American assumption of the Republic's indebtedness continued, Cáceres did everything he could to stabilize the internal affairs of the country and make it ultimately independent. The constitution was reformed. The power of the federal government was extended over the municipal *ayuntamientos* —without destroying the best features of local self-government. The presidential term was extended to six years. The office of vice president, hitherto a source of division, was abolished. A bureau of public works was established to take over the operations previously usurped by self-seeking foreign concessionaires. Public utilities, including port works, were turned over to public ownership.

Large-scale road building commenced, and sanitary facilities were built. For the first time the armed forces were systematically paid, fed, and clothed.

And for all these reforms, which necessarily involved a shift of power from private entrepreneurs to the government, Federico Velásquez also bore more than his share of denunciation. It was almost inevitable that the government's enemies, seeking some disinterested figurehead through which to channel its attack, should have turned to Horacio Vásquez. And it was almost as inevitable that General Vásquez, caught between his loyalty to his old comrade Ramón Cáceres and his idealistic ambition to lead the forces of "local self-government" in their "patriotic" opposition to "American Imperialism," should have become the unwitting agent of subversion. Jiménez, Morales, Luis Tejera, and other dissident exiles were constantly plotting for Cáceres' overthrow by violence, but no sooner would Vásquez be apprised of their willingness to resort to illegal and violent means than he would reluctantly break with them and communicate the impending danger to Cáceres in Santo Domingo. Cáceres, meanwhile, in keeping with his temperament, assumed that the Republic's prosperity was enough of a proof of the soundness of his (and Velásquez') policies to insure their safety.

In the summer of 1911, Luis Tejera, a young man motivated by little but the thwarting of his personal ambition to control the national guard, organized a band of assassins in the capital. On November 19 the President, though forewarned, took his customary evening drive, attended only by the head of his staff and a coachman. As their carriage swung into the Independencia, it passed two prominent citizens—Don Francisco J. Peynado and Don Juan Bautista Vicini Burgos—on the Malecón. They greeted Cáceres jovially, "You are a fine President, driving without an escort!" to which Cáceres replied in jest, "Damn the vagabonds!" A few minutes later, returning to Guibia, a small car and a wagon blocked the street. Cáceres was fatally wounded by a fusilade of shots. Staggering into the Peynado driveway, the mortally wounded President was carried into the American legation next door, where he died minutes later.

If it was "poetic justice" that Ramón Cáceres thus died, in precisely the same circumstances as the dictator to whom he had administered death twelve years before, then indeed is Poetry, in the Greek sense, subordinated to Justice, blind. For within a matter of weeks the Dominican Republic, in consequence of this heartless act, was reduced to the anarchy from which Cáceres had raised it with such heroic effort, an anarchy from which nothing but the unwanted hand of foreign intervention could now raise it.

To understand the American occupation that followed in the wake of this breakdown, it will be helpful to review Dominican-American relations since 1865. From the American point of view, it must be admitted that by the time policy makers in Washington had adopted a long-range program designed to help Dominicans help themselves, it was already too late to avoid implementing that help by force of arms. From the Dominican point of view, it is just as essential to recognize that internal anarchy, floatation of loans at ruinous rates that were never intended to benefit the people, and continuous bids for foreign intervention can hardly be blamed on outsiders. It is also necessary to examine the record in its historical framework rather than in the hindsight of present-day revulsion against "Yankee Imperialism," a policy in the mid-nineteenth century not recognized as such by either party, and rejected in Washington before World War II. Even in the heyday of the United States' "manifest destiny" to "protect" its weaker neighbors, when Cuba was being placed under a quasi protectorate and Panama was being carved out of Colombia to facilitate the construction of the Canal, it was the sabre rattler Theodore Roosevelt who had the imagination to pursue a course designed to make the Dominican Republic eventually strong and independent, whereas the do-nothing William Howard Taft permitted abuses to multiply, and the liberal Woodrow Wilson closed his eyes to both the disastrous accumulation of petty "incidents" and the ultimate folly of outright intervention.

In the whole unedifying spectacle of Dominican-American relations, then, the question is not who was "right" and who was "wrong." The fact of the matter is that the United States, when it was not entirely indifferent, yielded to a desultory appetite to swallow its helpless neighbor piecemeal (or at a single gulp); and that its helpless neighbor responded to this primitive appetite by alternately stimulating it and accommodating it. Farsighted men in both countries, sometimes men at the helm, opposed this cruel pastime. But for the most part there was little resistance in official American circles to letting predatory business interests shape policy, and very little resistance at any level of Dominican society to bartering the national heritage to the highest bidder.

We have already seen how Lincoln's Secretary of State unsuccessfully attempted to divert the great emancipator on the eve of the Civil War by delivering belligerent ultimatums to Washington's rivals among the powers in the Caribbean. No sooner was the war over and Lincoln dead than Secretary Seward returned to his obsession of acquiring a West Indian naval base. Setting sail for Santo Domingo, where he arrived with his son on January 15, 1866, Seward at once entered into negotiatoins with the more-than-willing Baez for the lease or purchase of Samaná Peninsula. These talks came to nothing when Seward's political foes in the Senate discovered that the Secretary's "agent" in Santo Domingo had once been a vociferous Confederate, and the matter was temporarily dropped. It was reopened two years later when terms for a ninety-nine-year lease were offered by Dominican President Cabral. Then Baez returned to power the same year, and that unscrupulous rascal, in a vain effort to save himself from financial ruin, lowered the ante considerably. Annexation of the entire country was now proposed.

Seward, whose purchase of Alaska from the slave-ridden Russians and support of republican self-government in Mexico had been in line with an enlightened policy of hemispheric solidarity under the

Monroe Doctrine, now suddenly went overboard for naked expansionism. Failing to get Senate support for the purchase of the Danish Virgin Islands, he now endeavored to sell President Johnson on the proposition of annexing Santo Domingo and Haiti at once, Cuba and Puerto Rico later. Baez was delighted. "Your idea," he wrote the American President, "is preferable to any other policy for this country. . . ." But even as Baez was anticipating the President's acquiescence by hoisting the American flag, the United States Senate, under the able leadership of the old Abolitionist Charles Sumner, was preparing to tell Johnson's successor, General Ulysses Grant, in no uncertain terms, that *any* treaty threatening however indirectly the re-exploitation of former Negro slaves was out.

In vain was Washington assured that "the Dominican people as one man long for annexation"; in vain was the instrument of annexation initialed; in vain was the American flag hoisted at Samaná and saluted by the local authorities; in vain did the lying Baez reassure his people that the United States was, after all, "a collection of free and independent republics, united by a common bond, each state possessing its own religion, language, habits, and customs"; in vain did he hold two phony plebiscites to reassure Washington that annexation was popular; and in vain did the desperate Grant plead, cajole, exaggerate, and threaten. "The resolution," thundered Sumner in one of the most famous and electrifying speeches ever delivered in America, "commits Congress to a dance of blood. As senator," he went on,

> as patriot, I cannot see my country suffer in its good name without an earnest effort to save it. Baez . . . is sustained in power by the Government of the United States that he may betray his country. . . . The island of San Domingo, situated in tropical waters and occupied by another race . . . never can become a permanent possession of the United States. You may seize it by force of arms or by diplomacy, where an able squadron does more than the Minister; the enforced jurisdiction cannot endure. . . . It is theirs by right of possession; by their sweat and blood mingling with the soil; by its burning sun and by unalterable lines of climate. Such is the ordinance of nature which I am not the first to rec-

ognize. San Domingo is the earliest of that independent group destined to occupy the Caribbean Sea toward which our duty is plain as the Ten Commandments. Kindness, benevolence, assistance, aid, help, protection, all that is implied in good neighborhood, this we must give freely, bountifully; but their independence is as precious to them as ours is to us and it is placed under the safeguard of natural laws which we cannot violate with impunity.

Shortly after this oration, President Grant, despite support from three commissioners who came back from the island with "news" that the Dominicans overwhelmingly favored annexation, received his first great defeat.

Early in 1873, as we have noted earlier, the merchandizing efforts entered a less reputable phase with the setting up of the Samaná Bay Company and Baez' success in selling his country to a group of out-and-out speculators. President González' cancellation of the concession in 1874 was a momentary setback for the freebooters on both sides, but Espaillat's fervent warning two years later, delivered in the form of an expression of disillusionment with Grant, went unheeded:

> Can you understand how bitterly they have suffered who had thought to find in the United States their perfect ideal of political institutions? Can you appreciate how sad and at the same time how repugnant a spectacle it has been to those who have admired the achievements which have created the political life of that great people to see one of their Presidents negotiating a "deal" with the Government of a small Republic—following the example proffered by a European Monarch, and without even having, as had the latter, for excuse the force of selfish interest?

Though President Heureaux made constant efforts to revive the Samaná deal—"Let your Government come and take it!" he once begged the McKinley administration—negotiations became inextricably entwined with attempts to free the Republic from its debt slavery to foreign bondholders. It was President Theodore Roosevelt in 1902 who determined to depart from the sterile and pusillanimous policy of invoking the Monroe Doctrine merely to warn off European powers, in favor of a constructive, long-range policy. Under this policy the foreign claims against the bankrupt Latin American countries were to be purchased, and the settlement of this single debt was to be negotiated by agreements involving the collection of import duties—then amounting to almost 95 per cent of all customs receipts—and their distribution in cooperation with the native governments. Failing to get the assent of the Senate to ratify the agreement he had made with President Morales, President Roosevelt authorized the immediate enactment of a *modus vivendi* under which 45 per cent of the revenues collected at the Dominican ports would be delivered to the Dominican government for its current expenses, the remainder to be deposited for eventual distribution among the government's creditors following ratification. This was the famous "Receivership of 1905" which, whatever its antecedents and ulterior motives, saved the Dominican Republic from bankruptcy—and from the division threatened by the several claimants to its $29,500,000 of foreign and internal debt. Had the arrangement been accepted in good faith by the Horacistas and Jimenistas alike, it is probable that the incentive to constant revolution would have been eliminated. The case for its acceptance was stated in 1907 by Emiliano Tejera, President Cáceres' foreign minister, as follows:

> What will happen if Congress does not accept the treaty? You know as well as I; it would mean the triumph of the speculators of former years; permanent civil war; the impossibility of paying off domestic or foreign creditors because all our resources will be expended in civil war; the discredit and the final downfall of the few good men in the country; the ruin of the Nation in every sense of the word.

On February 8, 1907, the convention making the receivership official was signed in Santo Domingo. On February 25 it was ratified by the United States Senate. On May 3, after bitter political recriminations by the Jimenistas, it was passed by the Dominican congress.

The return to anarchic conditions following President Cáceres' assassination—in ten months' time his successor, Eladio Victoria, had exhausted the government's surplus and, in violation of the convention, increased the public debt by $1,500,000—coincided with the succession of President Roosevelt by the weak President Taft. Secretary of State Root, a statesman, was in turn succeeded by Philander Knox, a lawyer who thought in terms of dollars rather than good will. As Sumner Welles put it:

> The liberation of Cuba, the practical assistance rendered the Dominican Republic without extorting material compensation in return thereof, the helpful and altruistic disposition demonstrated by the United States Government in the Central-American Conference held at Washington in 1908, and the patent sincerity of the declarations made by Secretary Root on behalf of his Government in his notable address at Rio de Janeiro in 1906, had all tended to create a friendly feeling of trust and respect towards the United States on the part of her southern neighbors.
>
> With the advent of Secretary Knox, however . . . the foreign policy of the United States was determined by the immediate requirements of a limited privileged class in the United States rather than by a true appreciation of the ultimate national interest.

The assumption was now made manifest that the Department of State, rather than the Dominican people or their government, must determine all policy—and enforce it. In the arrogant words of the American minister to Secretary Knox:

> Only complete control by our Government would permanently insure order and justice, but any degree of control would be beneficial; indeed, without our effective control, one administration here would be as good as another. Once having landed men for the protection of the custom-houses, in accordance with our rights under the convention, we might be able to dictate a policy beneficial to the country. The main evils to be remedied are: the absolute subservience of the courts; forced recruiting for the army; wholesale imprisonment without trial; peculation of public funds.

This was written on September 19, 1912. The first violation of Dominican sovereignty followed swiftly. Commissioners, escorted by a detachment of Marines, arrived on September 24 and dictated to President Victoria a series of "reforms" ranging from the relocation of the Haitian frontier to the removal from office of the President's nephew. The acceptance of even a few of these measures by the President had the immediate effect of gaining adherents for a revolution already launched against him in the Cibao and backed by General Vásquez. Advised that further conflict would precipitate American armed intervention, Vásquez worked out a compromise with Victoria and the American commissioners under which Adolfo A. Nouel, the archbishop of Santo Domingo, was elected by the congress to a two-year term as provisional president.

A man of charm and integrity, but no Padre Meriño, Archbishop Nouel attempted futilely to give both Horacistas and Jimenistas what they wanted. Taking advantage of Vásquez' good will and temporary retirement, the Jimenistas, under General Desiderio Arias, demanded that their faction be given full power. Quickly the Horacistas began to rearm. On March 31, 1913, the harassed Nouel resigned. Revolution broke out in September, following the failure of the new provisional president, General José Bordas Valdez, to secure the allegiance of either of the two parties.

President Woodrow Wilson had now succeeded Taft in Washington, and one of the first acts of his bumbling secretary of state, William Jennings Bryan, was to take sides in the Dominican dispute by bitterly censuring General Vásquez. Wilson had intended to break sharply with the "dollar diplomacy" of the Taft regime by refusing to identify state policy with commerce. "It is a very perilous thing," he had stated earnestly, "to determine the foreign policy of a nation in terms of material interests."

Unfortunately, the President's appointees in this field, from Bryan on down, were politicians, men completely incapable of understanding the abstract intellectual idealism of their chief—or of carrying it into practice. The incompetent Bryan began his Dominican fair deal by appointing the still more incompetent James Mark Sullivan minister to Santo Domingo. Sullivan's first act of incompetence—the first of a long line of such mistaken acts that were to plague American foreign policy into the second half of the twentieth century—was to support the reactionary *status quo* in its confrontation of a liberal opposition, simply because it is easier to deal with a government in power than with men seeking to overthrow it. "I am authorized to say to you, people of Monte Cristi," said the know-nothing Sullivan, landing there, "that in the opinion of the United States there is no grievance which now exists or which can exist which justifies resort to arms. The will of the people should prevail in this Republic and . . . the people can demand a fair ballot." Baseball, Sullivan advised Bryan blandly, should provide "a real substitute for the excitement of revolutions." In the forthcoming election, Sullivan advised that the United States take charge of the balloting, and he requested that the navy stand offshore to see that there was no cheating. Bryan backed up Sullivan's request, and there thus came about the first formal intervention in Dominican domestic affairs.

In the summer of 1914 the second incident occurred. While President Bordas was in Puerto Plata attempting to put down a local uprising, both sides were commanded by the captain of an American ship in the harbor not to bombard the city. When the President disregarded the order, the U.S.S. *Machias* shelled his camp.

With the election of Juan Isidro Jiménez to the presidency for the second time on December 5, 1914, a showdown became a certainty. Too weak to stand up openly to American pressure, Jiménez was smart enough to know that if he capitulated openly he would be opposed not only by the Horacista majority in congress, but by the dominant figures—General Arias and Federico Velásquez—in his own cabinet. Threatened with impeachment, Jiménez got off a frantic appeal for help to Secretary Bryan. Bryan backed him, and Bryan's successor in 1915, Robert Lansing, warned that troops might have to be landed soon to maintain order and to uphold the convention which, it was claimed, successive Dominican governments had now violated to the tune of $7,000,000.

As a matter of fact, American troops had already taken over in Haiti. With World War I already a year under way, Haiti was too "hot" to leave to chance, and rival arms. Germany had landed a few marines at Port-au-Prince during a disturbance in February of 1914 and was pursuing an aggressive policy in both parts of the island. In June of 1915 a French landing force virtually took over Cap Haïtien. The lynching of President V. G. Sam on July 27, following his butchery of 167 political hostages, provided the perfect setting for Rear Admiral William Caperton, acting on State Department orders, to call in a brigade of Marines and restore order in the blood-dazed country.

Across the border, meanwhile, new American demands were rapidly making Jiménez' position untenable. Faced with imminent insurrection, the President received Secretary Lansing's assurance that if he should request military aid he would get it. On May 1, 1916, President Jiménez was impeached by both houses of the congress "for violation of the Constitution and the laws." General Arias' troops now controlled the capital. The President was asked by Secretary Lansing to request aid. Jiménez hesitated. Marines began landing at the principal ports, and on May 7 Jiménez resigned. On May 13 Admiral Caperton arrived from Haiti on his flagship, the U.S.S. *Dolphin* and ordered General Arias to surrender. Though commanding many times the number of the seven hundred Marines so far landed, Arias—perhaps because he had heard about the machine guns with which his troops were not equipped—fled into the interior. When Colonel J. H. Pendleton's Fourth Regiment of Marines landed at Monte Cristi, bought up all twelve Model T Fords at the Ford agency, joined at Navarrete with Major Hiram Bearss, who had mounted a landing gun on a flatcar ahead of the railroad's four boxcars and run it through the La Cumbre tunnel from Puerto Plata, Santiago was outflanked. It fell on July 6, 1916, and General Arias surrendered. Admiral Caperton explained American intentions in the following terse communiqué:

> It is not the intention of the United States Government to acquire by conquest any territory in the Dominican Republic nor to attack its sovereignty, but our troops will remain here until all revolutionary

movements have been stamped out and until such reforms as are deemed necessary to insure the future welfare of the country have been initiated and are in effective operation.

The Dominicans countered by closing ranks. Picking a Jimenista who had lived so long outside the country that he could not possibly qualify as the yes-man the Americans were looking for, the leaders of the Horacista party in congress elected Dr. Francisco Henríquez y Carvajal provisional president. The Americans withheld recognition pending affirmation of two demands: (1) that the government recognize at once the United States' authority to collect and disburse all moneys; and (2) that the national army be replaced by a Dominican constabulary—in effect a police force under American tutelage. The new President refused to accept these demands unconditionally, and the Americans responded by cutting off all government revenues.

As autumn of 1916 approached, it became obvious that either the occupying forces would have to give in to Henríquez y Carvajal's "intransigeant" regime and withdraw, or assume the full responsibility by extending their police action to military government. Things had gone much too far for the first possibility even to be contemplated. Violent incidents involving Dominicans and Marines were on the increase. The Dominican press was beginning to fan the natural resentment of the citizenry into open hostility. The Henríquez y Carvajal government was still willing to negotiate, but it was too late. Secretary Lansing asked President Wilson for powers to resolve the crisis by radical means, and the President, now deeply preoccupied with the United States' imminent participation in World War I, reluctantly agreed. On November 29, Captain H. S. Knapp from his flagship in the harbor issued the proclamation which was to place the Dominican Republic under American military rule for the next eight years.

The American occupation, though never accepted by the vast majority of Dominicans except in a passive sense, met with little violent opposition. On the surface it accomplished a great deal of good. Peace, financial stability, economic growth, public works, military reform flourished as never before. But because it was founded upon a fundamental injustice—the arbitrary, illegal, and uncalled for usurpation of sovereignty by a great power over a small country— it accomplished nothing permanent. The political coming of age of the Dominicans was merely postponed. Suspicion, resentment, cynicism, repressed feelings, and in some areas lawlessness festered underground. An efficient machinery of repression, the nucleus of a police state, was bequeathed to those inclined to profit by such a mechanism. The image of the United States as the protector of the inviolability of the Pan-American sovereign states—so eloquently projected by Wilson himself in his writings and speeches—was tarnished for decades to come.

Captain (later Rear Admiral) Harry S. Knapp, an able governor and a good man, carried out his orders. An order that officers of the Marine Corps must hold the portfolios of interior and war soon led to the resignation of the other members of the Henríquez y Carvajal cabinet. The admiral found himself heading a government most of whose members knew nothing of Dominican affairs and sensibilities, and could not even speak the language of the country. Knapp can hardly be blamed either for the fact that the war in Europe deprived the Second Brigade (Marines) of its ablest officers, leaving unseasoned men of lower rank to command. Nor was it surprising that outstanding Dominicans refused to be trained as officers of the newly organized national constabulary, leaving the cadres to be filled with Americans—or native riffraff.

There was nothing hypocritical in Admiral Knapp's determination to deal with the Dominicans in a spirit of friendly conciliation. For the most part he succeeded as well as could be expected. But in the two eastern provinces of Seybo and San Pedro de Macoris, "resistance" and "retaliation" became chronic. Whether the "gavilleros," as the guerillas called themselves, were "patriots" or "bandits" depended, and still depends, on one's point of view. The "gavilleros," under such swashbuckling leaders as Dios Olivorio,* Vicentico, and Chacha, took full advantage of the sparsely populated, rolling, and (in places) densely thicketed terrain. The Marines had to rely on superior organization and fire power, and, in 1919, on the six Jennies of the First Air Squadron, based on a sugar plantation near Consuelo, which served both as effective spotters and improvised dive bombers. Especially in and around the village of Hato Mayor, which changed hands several times, the fighting was savage. And it was in this sector that a few American officers indulged in retaliatory acts of wanton cruelty and sadism that were to be remembered (and imitated) long after the arrest and subsequent suicide of Captain Charles F. Merkel, a German-born former enlisted man who was a principal instigator of the "counter-terror." The "final pacification" of the sector that took place in 1921 as plans for the withdrawal of the occupation were already under way, involved mass line-ups. The male population, according to Colonel Robert D. Heinl's Marine Corps history, was passed in review at night under floodlights while informers, carefully hidden in tents, picked out "known bandits":

> After five months of the "cordon system," nine successful roundups had been carried out, and more than 600 courtroom convictions for banditry resulted. Following this crackdown, the cordons were discontinued because of the resentment aroused by such methods among those who were innocent. General Lee, the Military Governor, then proclaimed a two months' period of amnesty, during which bandits were encouraged to surrender, and, simultaneously, five special anti-bandit groups were trained from among Dominicans who had suffered at bandit hands.

On the positive side, the military government established the beginnings of a civil service and of a responsible audit and control of public works. Experts in agriculture encouraged the growing of more varied crops with modern implements, though little was done

---

* This was the famous "Liborio" who claimed to be a reincarnation of God, set up his own "religion," and built up a following which refused to recognize any laws but their own. The cult persisted into 1963 when Dominican troops, charging Haitian backing, wiped out a rebellious enclave of its followers at Palma Sola.

to spur large-scale farming and nothing at all to break up the vast, untilled *haciendas* and distribute land more equably among the largely landless peasant class. A sanitation system and sanitary laws were introduced. Land titles, in a state of chaos over the centuries, were searched and legitimized. The floating debt was scaled down from $12,000,000 to $3,500,000. Education, following the recommendations of a committee of distinguished Dominicans, was drastically overhauled: teachers were paid promptly, new schools were established, one hundred thousand pupils were enrolled. Road building, which had come to a standstill after the Cáceres period, began again: Monte Cristi was for the first time linked with the capital via Santiago, and the east-west road along the south coast was partially completed.

Admiral Knapp's replacement in 1918 by Rear Admiral Thomas Snowden—"Don Juan Isidro" Snowden the Dominicans called him, in reference to their unhappy experiences with the vacillating Jiménez—brought the period of relative tolerance and good will to an end. The Navy Department, engrossed with the war in Europe, was satisfied to let the military government in Santo Domingo drift into a frank dictatorship. Freedom of speech and of the press were snuffed out. The various committees of able Dominicans who had advised Knapp resigned. When Snowden was asked for a timetable under which the occupation could be gradually eliminated, he advised the Department of State to declare that "a minimum period of twenty years" would be in order. Meanwhile, however, protests over Washington's highhanded policy were beginning to multiply throughout Latin America, and indeed in the United States itself. Samuel Gompers, first president of the American Federation of Labor, was only the most prominent of those voices that had been clamoring at President Wilson for years to withdraw the troops. Late in 1920, following his defeat over American participation in the League of Nations, the message seems to have come through to Wilson at last. It was as though no one had thought to bring up the subject with him before, and perhaps this was the case. Turning to his new secretary of state, Bainbridge Colby, who had informed him of the ugly situation, the stricken President authorized steps leading to immediate withdrawal.

The problem facing the military government in 1921 was to find a group of recognized patriots in the country to whom the power could be handed over. For months extremists had been branding anyone even seen talking with an American as a traitor. Yet to yield to the extremists' slogan of "Evacuation, pure and simple!" would not only have meant turning over the country to a mob rule worse than that building up in 1916; it would have meant undoing most of the good works accomplished over six years, leaving without validity all the thousands of contracts, concessions, and laws on which the economy of the country now depended, and ruining in the process thousands of innocent, industrious Dominicans. Those leaders from all parties who were to form the first negotiating committee—Archbishop Nouel, General Vásquez, Federico Velásquez, Dr. Ramón Baez, Enrique Jiménez, Francisco J. Peynado, Dr. José María Cabral y Baez, Justice Rafael Justino Castillo, Tulio Cestero, Jacinto de Castro, Judge Manuel de Jesús Troncoso de la Concha, General Juan Francisco Sánchez, and Manuel de Jesús Lluberes—were aided in their task by the election of Warren G. Harding to the American presidency and by his appointment of the able Charles Evans Hughes as secretary of state.

Harding, unlike Hughes, was no statesman, but he had campaigned with Wilson's more obvious blunders constantly in his sights, and he had no intention of living with the worst of them. He began by appointing in Snowden's place an officer who might stand a chance of gaining the respect of the Dominicans. Rear Admiral Samuel S. Robison's first move was to issue a fairly conciliatory convention of evacuation. It was not conciliatory enough to satisfy the committee of Dominicans named above, who promptly resigned. But thanks largely to the persistence of Velásquez, Peynado, and General Vásquez himself, a new plan was drawn up which allowed for the selection of a provisional president who would govern, along with the residual military government, until a constitutional president could be elected in free balloting supervised by the Dominicans themselves. Sumner Welles, appointed by President Harding as high commissioner to negotiate the political details of the transition, traveled throughout the country and reported back to Washington that the evacuation plan was approved by a great majority of the people. Juan Bautista Vicini Burgos, a nonpolitical sugar millionaire of Italian extraction, was agreed upon as the provisional president and was installed on October 21, 1922. Dominican citizens now hastened to enroll as cadets and were trained, under the direction of Richard M. Cutts, U.S.M.C., to take over the Policía Nacional Dominicana. A central electoral board was created, and two parties—one headed by General Vásquez and Federico Velásquez, the other by Francisco J. Peynado—began to campaign.

So obviously overwhelming was the national popularity of General Vásquez that Peynado, a professional man with no following in the countryside, seriously considered withdrawing from the race. Prevailed upon not to deal the electoral system a body blow at the outset, Peynado put up at least a perfunctory fight. More than one hundred thousand voters went to the polls on March 15, 1924, and throughout the country the balloting was uncoerced and orderly. Vásquez was elected president and his Alianza party gained twenty-five out of thirty-one members of the House of Deputies and ten out of twelve members of the National Senate. On July 13 Vásquez was inaugurated, and the American flag which had waved over the Ozama Fortress for almost eight years was replaced by the Dominican colors. On September 18 the last American Marine left the Republic. It seemed, as Sumner Welles said in the concluding sentence of his monumental history of the preceding epoch, that "a new era of liberty and independence had commenced."

IX

Total Eclipse, 1925-60

Dictatorship Unlimited Under Trujillo and His Family

On a hilltop commanding San Cristobal, birthplace of Rafael Leon-idas Trujillo Molina, there now stands a building that resembles a cheap, three-story parking garage set beside a filling station and capped by an archaic airport control tower. A dozen years after its construction it was already falling into decay, its surface concrete mouldering, the pavement of its patio split by cracks, the elaborate terraced gardens gone to weed and cactus. Entering by a massive door and crossing one of the splendid parquet floors flanked by intricately carved mahogany wainscotting, one is confronted by a staircase that appears to rest upon a dung-colored doughnut the size of a bomber wheel. Six gigantic bedchambers, to which this staircase and a brace of stainless steel elevators lead, stand empty. With recessed, half-domed ceilings, "supported" by pink, blue, or green pilasters and appliquéd in gesso with military emblems, victory wreaths, acanthus, gold braid, rosettes, egg and dart in six different colors, and imitation Grecian urns spouting blue foam, these chambers are lighted by cheap plastic chandeliers that would be rejected out of hand by the interior decorator of an automat. Dwarfing these, and adjacent salons whose

marble floors, imported from Italy, ill consort with an ensemble presumably modeled on St. Louis bordellos of the 1890's, are fifteen
outsize bathrooms. Walled and floored in imported mosaic featuring
octopuses and other tropical fish, one of them is equipped with
six-foot-high blue mirrors. The bidets and washstands are of red
porphyry. The revolving toothbrush stands resemble gold. And the
cedar closets, like those in the bedrooms, are not only lined with
aromatic cedar but contain hundreds of empty, perfectly fitted
drawers, and drawers within drawers, handmade—one's guide is
proud to explain—of a precious wood secured against common use by
constitutional edict. A smoking room, with sculptured Buddhas leap-
frogging the ceiling, and oriental lettering reliefed in bamboo on
scores of safe-size humidors built into the four walls, is not at all out
of key with the prevailing *décor*. But the mammoth kitchen, with its
functional stainless steel sinks, spits, ovens, electric washers and
driers, mixers, fans, king-size freezers, and air conditioning units, is
saved from violating the canon of bad taste by a tiny electric clock
in the form of a red teapot, winking high and naked on one wall.
There remains a polished-marble chapel that resembles a Victorian
bathroom and a mural of rustic Dominican *chiquitas* (all white)
being given roses by simpering *campesinos*.*

This atrocious palace was never occupied, even for one night. No
one seems to know why. There was never any furniture in it. Two or
three typical parties were thrown, at which the elevators presumably
ran and the gigantic bars groaned with champagne and cognac, and
that was all. Since those who paid for the millions of hours of sweated
labor that went into its construction were never intended to enter it,
its purpose and cost were not a matter of public record. The architect,
who had previously built himself a landlocked "cruiser," complete
with blue concrete "waves," a few blocks from the national palace,
generously declines to take credit for providing totalitarian dictator-

---

* This mural is the work of one Vela Zanetti, an imported painter working the
debased Mexican tradition, who filled the dictator's cathedral with technicolored angels
and posturing saints.

ship with its perfect visual imagery. The *real* creator of "El Cerro" (the word, with one less *r* spells zero), and of dozens of other eyesores that now disfigure the country—from the "Peace" Monument at Santiago to the "Altagracia" Cathedral at Higüey—is not modest architect-engineer Henry Gazón Bona, staring out of his monograph on these accomplishments in a photograph that accentuates his Goering-like Air Force major's cap; the *real* author of these memorials

> to the resurrection of peace and civilization and eternal beauty [Gazón insists] is the protector, originator and director of *everything;* meriting for his abundant and fruitful genius, in addition to his other resplendent denominations, the title of First Architect of the Nation: Rafael L. Trujillo Molina, Benefactor of the Fatherland.

The man for whom this and other characteristic monuments were to be erected was born in San Cristobal October 24, 1891, in most modest circumstances. His official biographers' claim that he came of Spanish military stock on his father's side and of a French marchioness on his mother's is false. His enemies' insistence that his paternal grandfather was a police spy for the Spaniards under La Gándara and that his grandmother was a Haitian, is possibly more accurate but equally irrelevant. As a child he collected bottle caps (in lieu of medals, a later addiction), from which he acquired the nickname "Chapita." As a young man he became a telegraph operator and private policeman (possibly an informer) for one of the sugar companies he was later to acquire. Ernest Gruening asserts that in early military government days Trujillo was convicted for offenses of petty theft and forgery; but if this were so there is no evidence for it, because in time Trujillo was able to destroy incriminating documents and rewrite history as he chose.

When Customs Inspector James J. McLean, an old friend of the Trujillo family, was appointed by the Marines to be a major in the Dominican constabulary, he took the young Trujillo along with him as guide in the campaign against the eastern "gavilleros." If he served under Captain Charles Merkel before that sinister officer's disgrace and suicide, shooting down compatriots or tying them to horses' tails, the proof, on both sides, has been "lost." According to Marine Corps records, Lt. Trujillo (he received his commission and took the oath on January 11, 1919) had a clean, uneventful record of "capable" service, with little or no combat duty—a bill of comparative health which Galíndez confirms. In 1921, under the sponsorship of Lieutenant Colonel (later Lieutenant General) Thomas E. Watson, he received his formal training at the Haina Academy and took part in skirmishes against the "bandits" at La Noria, an engagement cited with praise by Watson but subsequently and suspiciously removed from the Dominican records by Trujillo himself.

In the years of confusion and gradual return to effective self-government that followed the Marines' withdrawal, Trujillo rose rapidly in the national police force. For his work as administrator of the northern department, he attracted the favorable attention of President Vásquez. "Panegyrists and enemies alike," says Galíndez, "admit that Trujillo did an effective administrative job as Chief of Police." If there was suspicion that he had a hand in informing the husband of his immediate superior's lover—an action which led to the assassination of Major Cesar Lora, and young Captain Trujillo's spectacular leap in grade to lieutenant colonel—no one was willing or able to prove it. If he made a small fortune on the uniforms and side arms that were his to distribute, that was hardly a practice without precedent. If his appointment in 1928 as brigadier general and chief of staff to the newly renamed National Army came about as a result of systematically exposing the shortcomings of his superiors—well, could anyone deny that those superiors *were* incompetent? If one of his young officers, Lieutenant Rafael Espaillat, in a fit of visionary inspiration renamed a small square in San Francisco de Macoris "Trujillo Square," who was General Trujillo to penalize excessive loyalty? Was not this the affirmative interpretation of the doctrine he had learned so well from his masters—that military rule cannot bear criticism?

Another doctrine he had noted approvingly—the Marines' summary treatment of offenders against their authority—had always been part of Rafael Trujillo's very nature; and being uninhibited by any qualms of Calvinistic conscience or Anglo-Saxon respect for civil rights, he far surpassed in ruthlessness his generally good-natured mentors.

Juan Bosch, in his study of the dictator's psychology, makes a great deal of the frustration the young Trujillo must have felt in being excluded from the homes of even the indigent "aristocracy" by their centuries-old caste tradition. If this was what drove Trujillo, he must soon have found other spurs to his ambition, for his revenge upon the exclusive "Club Union," when it blackballed him, was complete. He opened this campaign by getting an uncontested divorce from Aminta Ledesma, mother of the not yet notorious Flor de Oro, and taking as his second wife a poor blue blood, Bienvenida Ricardo. With her help, and that of Jacinto B. Peynado (who was to be repayed with the puppet presidency of 1938-40), he finally got himself elected to the haughty circle. Once in, it was a matter of months before the cunning General was able to sponsor membership for enough of his fellow officers to have himself elected club president. This might have satisfied a less vindictive temperament, but not Trujillo's. Not only were the old Dons now "advised" by the secret police to get out and found a new club for themselves—which they did; they were also instructed that the name of the new club should be "Club Presidente Trujillo"—which it promptly was.

The stage had already been set for the young General to extend his consuming appetite for power into the political sphere. In 1929 the fading Vásquez, though alarmed by an incipient revolt taking shape in the Cibao under the leadership of Rafael Estrella Ureña, was obliged to visit the United States for surgical treatment. Vásquez had ruled with predictable honesty in the six years since the last American soldiers left the country. He had also respected the rights of individuals, even when they had attacked him virulently and mendaciously in the press. But Vásquez had done little to counter the popular impression that he was making no major move without consulting his American friends; and he had done nothing at all to put an end to the murderous personal feuding between aging but still powerful Horacista and Jimenista politicians.

Trujillo, seeing his opportunity, at once began transferring weapons from the national arsenal to the rebels' stronghold in Santiago. So covertly was this done, and so seemingly sincere were the pledges of allegiance with which he reassured the old man on his return in January of 1930, that Vásquez' suspicions were allayed. On the eve of his campaign for re-election to the presidency, Vásquez' popularity was still immense. But acting through two distinguished civilian friends—Roberto Despradel and Rafael Vidal—Trujillo was able to persuade the Americans in Santo Domingo that the rebels might be right in charging that Vásquez' efforts to perpetuate himself in office violated a fundamental Dominican tradition.

By the time the Americans sensed that behind the smoke screens of "democratic tradition" and the "rebels' right to rebel" stood the ominously immobile figure of the chief of staff, it was too late to ask who he was or what was at stake. On February 24 the United States minister, Charles B. Curtis, and his third secretary, John Moors Cabot, alarmed by the approach of Estrella Ureña's forces, had offered asylum to Vásquez. Receiving telephoned assurance from the Ozama barracks of Trujillo's unwavering loyalty, the Americans concurred in Vásquez' desire to confer there with his military chief. Trujillo, too astute to make a martyr of the brave old general or to alienate the Americans by revealing his game in advance, assured Vásquez that troops were already on the march to intercept the rebels. By the time the rebels reached the city unopposed, it was too late for Vásquez to claim that he had been betrayed. Trujillo, who had already promised the gullible Americans that he would maintain strict political "neutrality," was now in a position to make good his promise, first by standing by while the rebels occupied the city, and then by simply taking back the arms which he had secretly given Estrella Ureña and returning them to the federal arsenal!

On February 27 General Vásquez and Estrella Ureña confronted each other at the American legation, and on March 3 Congress accepted the resignation of President Vásquez and Vice President Alfonseca. Estrella Ureña was inaugurated provisional president. In four months, it was agreed, a constitutional election would be held.

Trujillo's moves, in these four months, were calculated with foresight and executed with perfect deception. The Vásquez party, which was now rallying strongly behind the candidacies of Federico Velásquez and Angel Morales, was first rendered impotent by a decree ordering that all arms be surrendered to the new government. The American State Department, which had finally come to the conclusion that Trujillo's own candidacy would be "undesirable," was thrown off guard by his promise not to seek office. The time had now come for Estrella Ureña's pay-off. The *Confederación* that was backing him suddenly decided that Estrella Ureña would make a better vice presidential candidate. Could Trujillo, as a "good democrat," now refuse the candidacy for the presidential post that the "people" were forcing upon him? Of course he could not! In vain did Estrella Ureña now plead with the State Department to issue a statement denouncing Trujillo. Curtis was instead advised by Washington "not to impair in any way your relations with him [Trujillo]," but to make an appeal "in a most friendly spirit." Ignorant of this appeasement, Velásquez and Morales now launched their campaign under the brave slogan, *"No puede ser ... por ladrón de caballos!"*

"The period succeeding General Trujillo's entry into the Presidential campaign," wrote Charles A. Thomson in a subsequent Foreign Policy Association report, "witnessed the death or mysterious disappearance of a great number of his opponents. These included former cabinet ministers, ex-Senators, leading politicians, journalists, ranchers, business men, students and labor leaders." The instrument for this wholesale house cleaning, named after the enterprising Forty-second Company of the American Marine Corps, was "La 42." The leader of these storm troops was a gangster type of Italian extraction named Miguel Angel Paulino. He employed as his *Carro de la*

Muerte a red Packard driven by an ex-convict; and when the Chauffeurs' Union defied this murderous rule of the streets, Paulino promptly invaded its headquarters and had himself named union boss.

Whether the State Department's qualms were quieted by a visit from Rafael Brache, the Dominican minister in Washington, who assured the acting secretary that Candidate Trujillo was "very clever, intelligent and honest," Curtis was able to report that although the opposition had instructed its members to abstain from voting in the terror-ridden atmosphere, "I have the honor to confirm my report that there were no disorders during the day of the elections." To be sure, Curtis added, the 223,851 votes cast for Trujillo and Estrella Ureña greatly exceeded the total number of eligible voters in the country.

As for the President-elect, there was barely time to jail Velásquez, drive Morales out of the country, and turn the demoralized remnants of the opposition over to La 42, before an unforeseen opponent struck—and in striking presented Trujillo with a heaven-sent opportunity to start building on his own from the ground up.

> Mounting the hurricane to pitch his tent
> He gave Columbus' capital his name;
> They built his monuments for ten per cent
> Of the deceit, the profit, and the shame.*

On September 3, 1930, eighteen days after Trujillo had taken office, the most devastating hurricane in the history of the West Indies struck Santo Domingo City. Of an eighty thousand population, twenty-five hundred were counted dead, eight thousand injured, and many other thousands lost. Only the old colonial part of the city was spared; the poor sections were leveled. Although Trujillo seems to have panicked in the first days of the aftermath, asking the United States to send a Marine detachment to maintain order, and even calling on poverty-stricken Haiti for help, he soon attacked the disaster

---

* "Dictator," from Selden Rodman's *The Amazing Year* (New York, 1946).

with characteristic energy and turned it to his own benefit. Generous aid from the Red Cross and other foreign agencies could be spent without accounting. Other millions were raised on public credit. Those with property were ordered to rebuild at once. Those without became the dictator's debtors. All constitutional guarantees were suspended for the duration of the emergency. La 42 made gas-drenched bonfires of the victims—and of how many others no one will ever know.

The time had now come to master the nation's oldest problem—its crushing indebtedness to foreign claims. The treasury was empty, and $3,000,000 a year still had to be diverted from the national budget to service the bonds. Revenues, which had hit a peak of $15,385,000 in 1930, dropped to $7,350,000 in 1931. Trujillo began by slashing expenses—except the army's budget, which was raised to 11.5 per cent—drastically. Only two high schools in the entire country, for example, were permitted to stay open. The United States helped by diverting to him $1,500,000 from customs revenues, and by practically suspending payments on the sinking fund of its loans. By employing American financiers, like Joseph E. Davies, the Democratic party angel, as his negotiators in place of Dominicans, Trujillo got his way with President Franklin D. Roosevelt's secretary of state, Cordell Hull. While ten years were to pass before the signing of the Hull-Trujillo agreement of September 24, 1940, ending the customs convention, and another seven before the foreign debt would be entirely erased from the books, the road to solvency was now open.

Much more, of course, than foreign loans and deferments was required to put the Dominican budget in balance—even if the massive program of public works, economic development, and family fortune building that now followed had never been undertaken. What paid for all this? Essentially, the Dominican people paid for it, by submitting to one of the most crushing burdens of taxation ever devised. All of it, or almost all of it, was hidden. A graduated income tax, on the American model, had never existed in the Dominican Republic, and Trujillo did not introduce one.* Instead, the billions required for these enterprises came out of the pockets of the worker, the farmer, the small businessman (in the end, there were no large businessmen except the dictator and his proliferating family). This despoilment was painless. It took the form of price increases, taxes on everything imported or manufactured locally, and "contributions" sufficient to siphon off what remained. *As the standard of living of the country rose,* following the introduction of machines, efficiency measures, a speed-up in human productivity, and expanding foreign markets, *the standard of living of the average Dominican either remained the same or dropped.* Two thirds of the population continued to produce little and buy almost nothing. At late as 1958 there were only 58,000 radios, 2,000 television sets, and 7,150 automobiles in the entire country. Out of the indirect taxation Trujillo found the cash to finance Dominican industry's startling growth. Early attempts on the part of merchants to offset the hidden taxes brought prompt jail sentences. When a match factory in Puerto Plata shut down, Trujillo at once forced it to reopen and announced that any further shutdowns would be met by expropriation. Small landowners on the borders of expanding sugar plantations were simply evicted without any legal procedure or compensation at all. The proletarian status of once independent farmers on these and other large *haciendas* approached that of slave labor. Widely publicized minimum-wage laws and increased hourly payments never kept pace with the rising prices of essential foods and clothing. But the expansion of the nation's physical facilities was staggering to behold.

Trujillo's internal financing, according to an American economist working for the Dominican government in 1963, was "astonishingly intricate and sophisticated." Protection for new enterprises with

---

* As early as 1918 Otto Schoenrich had written: "The financial system of Santo Domingo is characterized by an inequitable mode of obtaining public revenue, whereby the burden of supporting the state is thrown upon the poorest classes in the form of indirect taxes upon articles of necessary consumption, and wherein taxation of property . . . according to economic capacity plays no part."

the protection tapering off, was one key. Capacity to sell uneconomic enterprises to the government *at a profit* and then buy them back for almost nothing when international prices rose and they were making money, was another. The tobacco monopoly was fantastically profitable, and so was the sugar trust for which Trujillo had borrowed $40,000,000 from commercial banks in the United States in order to buy off his competitors and consolidate with one of the most modern plants in existence. He paid off this $40,000,000 over ten years, half of it in a single lump sum.

Was it true, as some of his detractors insisted, that the bulk of the dictator's profits, perhaps as much as a billion dollars, were banked or invested abroad? No one will deny that Trujillo had become in the fifties one of the world's two or three richest individuals. According to *Time* magazine, his investments in the United States and Puerto Rico alone amounted to $100,000,000. But it was inconceivable, the American economist said, that Trujillo could have removed more than $3,000,000 annually over a thirty-year period into accounts overseas:

> Look at *Hacienda Fundación* with its thousands of blooded cattle and *Engombé* with its three-hundred brood mares and huge plantation houses! Look at the country's incomparable road net, all built in those thirty years. Look at Stone & Webster's superb power grid with its perfected generators from Barahona to Higüey. He paid $5,000,000 for that alone, supplying 100,000 customers as against 50,000 when he took over. Consider the $5,000,000 he sank into sisal, cotton and cotton-textile manufacturing right after World War II (for this he literally created $5,000,000 out of thin air, first borrowing it, then issuing bonds against the discounted notes, and then selling these to the central bank which was required to issue $5,000,000 in new currency. The tax on textiles which he then enacted into law not only protected his cotton goods but brought the government additional revenues, thus ultimately helping to pay off the bonds). Look at the sanitation and water-supply systems which until three years ago supplied the capital and the other cities adequately. Look at the $20,000,000 port and docking facilities he built in Santo Domingo, Puerto Plata and Barahona, where none existed before, and in San Pedro de Macoris. Or the $18,000,000 International

Airport, or the $40,000,000 worth of offices and auditoriums at the Fair Ground. Or the multi-million dollar irrigation systems, some of which worked; the dozens of million-dollar hotels and hospitals; not to mention the millions of dollars worth of (useless) Vampire Jets he bought from England. All of this survived here. None of it was salted away.

Before considering the human cost of this incontrovertible accomplishment, let us look at it, industry by industry, in a little more detail.

Sugar. Under Trujillo, the Dominican Republic became virtually a one-crop country. Exports of sugar by 1956 were valued at $49,800,000. By 1957 sugar accounted for 49 per cent of the country's total volume of exports, paid 27.7 per cent of all salaries and wages, employed 73 per cent of the working population. Only Cuba exceeded its 993,172 tons of annual production, and although Cuba continued to receive the lion's share of the United States preferential quota, thus forcing the Dominican Republic to sell at the world price (35 per cent less), Trujillo skillfully manipulated the small Dominican share his way so as to force Dominican competitors out of business. He had begun to buy up sugar mills as far back as the thirties. In 1946-48 work began on the giant plant at Rio Haina, soon to be the hub of the twelve-mill complex the dictator controlled. Of the remaining four, only the very profitable South Porto Rico Sugar Company at La Romana was at all significant; and perhaps it was permitted to remain in American hands only because its exclusive compound of executives' bungalows provided such a convenient symbol of "imperialism." But without the seasonal importation of an army of cane cutters from Haiti, ready to work hard for substandard wages, Trujillo's sugar industry would never have shown profits.

Coffee. Although the $32,800,000 crop in the peak year of 1956 made coffee the Republic's second biggest export commodity, Trujillo himself showed little interest in it, and in fact destroyed many plantations to provide grazing lands for his more favored cattle monopoly.

Cocoa. Third in exports, with a $23,889,261 crop in its peak year, cocoa provides a sidelight on the dictator's business methods. Three Poles were encouraged to build a chocolate factory at Puerto Plata in 1946. Subsidized with the kickback from a 28 per cent export tax on the beans, it prospered. By the time it was making $1,000,000 a year, Trujillo "bought" it at a bargain price. By selling it, and rebuying every two or three years, he made big cash profits. But in addition to this he was able to clear $2,000,000 a year by the simple device of having the whole $2.10 per bag tax at the Puerto Plata embarkation point placed in a cigar box instead of going to the treasury.

Tobacco. The only other sizeable export crop (apart from bananas, which Trujillo left in American hands), tobacco became a Trujillo monopoly early in the thirties. In expropriating an Italian magnate with a controlling interest, Trujillo had to turn to the United States for help when Mussolini threatened to shell Dominican ports over this action. By 1956 exports of tobacco amounted to $5,000,000.

During the war, Trujillo was able to export great quantities of meat to the United States, using American technical assistance to build several merchant ships for this profitable trade. But the livestock industry did not attain major importance, and after the war reverted to supplying the local market. Salt, gypsum, and iron ore, likewise profitable mainly in the domestic market, were among the earliest Trujillo monopolies. A partial list of the other investments in which the dictator and his family had a controlling share would include milk, alcohol, beer, firewood, pitch pine, baking, printing, fishing, shoes, marble, airplane and shipping transportation, matches, industrial gases, construction materials, cement, glass bottling, small arms manufacture, electric batteries, slaughterhouses and refrigeration plants, cigar and cigarette manufacture, hardware and plumbing, banking, rents, medicines, rice, sweets, sisal, and paint. The last two were handled with special tenderness. All export produce, it was decreed, must be packed in sisal containers. Every Dominican was required to paint his house twice yearly. Arismendi Trujillo was given control over the export of bananas, plantains, and poultry. Pedro worked the charcoal racket. Brother Romeo, appropriately, acquired the concession for prostitution.

It would be a mistake to suppose that none of these flourishing enterprises benefited the Dominican economy. The terms state monopoly and Trujillo monopoly are interchangeable in the years 1930-60. An analogy might be the enormous increase in industrial production in Russia after Lenin, almost none of which trickled down to the average Russian. Profits in the Dominican Republic, instead of going into armaments, went into the Trujillo family bank accounts. But in both cases the nation's physical plant—its capacity to produce—got built. And in both cases the consumer, if he could ever manage to channel production his way, would be the ultimate beneficiary.

How much of all this would have been accomplished anyway, under a democratic regime or a benevolent socialist one? Certainly high prices in the postwar world market in coffee, sugar, tobacco, and cocoa—these accounted for 86.8 per cent of all Dominican exports by 1956—helped. The repeal, through a 1934 constitutional amendment, of a prohibition imposed upon the government's power to tax export commodities, helped also. So did Trujillo's adroit manipulation of reserves of foreign exchange. Probably Germán Ornes sums it up fairly when he says:

> It is impossible . . . to determine whether the progress of the country would have been greater had it been governed by a democratic regime during the last twenty-seven years. The obvious advantages of a dictatorship in making trains run on time, averting strikes and forcing people to work hard are too well-known to be repeated here. . . .

The political superstructure through which Trujillo sought to give the illusion that the Republic was being democratically governed was so transparently fraudulent that few were taken in by it, even abroad.

Trujillo himself was titular president from 1930 to 1934 and again from 1934 to 1938. Two puppet presidents were in office from 1938 to 1940 and from 1940 to 1942—Jacinto B. Peynado and Manuel de Jesús Troncoso de la Concha. The Generalissimo dispensed with this fiction for the ten years that followed, his fourth and fifth terms running from 1942 to 1947 and from 1947 to 1952. Brother Hector was the puppet from 1952 on, his vice president after 1957 being Joaquin Balaguer. Hector, it was said, ·read the official *La Nación* each morning to see what his decisions of the day before had been.

Until 1955 Trujillo saw no reason to discard the constitution he had inherited from his predecessors. Its separated legislature, executive, and judiciary, together with an elaborate bill of rights, proved no obstacle to him. In fact the new constitution of 1955 diverged from the old one mainly in "guaranteeing" individual liberties even more vehemently. It also declared Communism incompatible with civilization; sanctified the official Partido Dominicano; and stated hopefully that the Generalissimo's growing list of titles might never be revoked.

In practice, of course, all of this was window dressing. The single party, unlike its Soviet counterpart, did not run the country. It told the people when and how to vote, staged mass rallies and "spontaneous demonstrations" to cheer Trujillo. Its million-and-a-half adult members would meet periodically in modernistic headquarters in the fifty-four principal cities and towns, under the insignia "*Rectitud, Libertad, Trabajo, Moralidad*" (Trujillo's initials). The docile membership served as a vast body of informers—on the unorganized minority and on each other.

Acting in response to the strings pulled by Trujillo, the party exercised its exclusive "right" to fill vacancies in congress. Every congressman was obliged to sign his own resignation before taking office. Germán Ornes served two years in this meek body and does not recall "a single argument over the passage of a bill." He testifies also that the courts consistently denied political offenders the right to confront their accusers and subjected them to double jeopardy. Ornes' father, for example, acquitted a young student twice, only to have the government remove him from the magistrate's chair and appoint a judge who finally did condemn the young man.

In foreign policy as in economics Trujillo followed no ideological goal. The class struggle, and dictatorship in the name of the workers, that gave Communism its rationale, meant no more to Trujillo than did the zeal for racial supremacy that drove National Socialism toward world conquest. Only the *means,* the techniques of suppression developed so skillfully by these two modern totalitarian systems, interested Trujillo. "Despite the seduction of impractical theories," he wrote, "beautifully presented Utopias, purely ideological considerations . . . and the pressures exerted to sway me in their behalf—my sense of the practical always prevailed over the fantastic." Power for its own sake, personal aggrandizement over men, and possessions—concentrated, hoarded, and flaunted in a vulgar public display—were the beginning and the end of Trujillo's drive. And since circumstances made it impossible for him to exert power directly over other nations, even over his weak neighbor on Hispaniola, Trujillo's foreign policy took the form of *security:* preventing, so far as possible, subversion from abroad; concentrating armaments so formidable that no other Latin American power could threaten him; and guarding the rugged western frontier against traditional infiltrations with the only weapon that could effectively seal it—a reign of terror.

In the thirties, when Hitler was riding high, Trujillo hinted to him that submarine bases might be available; but as soon as the United States entered the conflict openly, Trujillo ranged himself firmly against the Axis, widely publicized his offers of asylum to Spanish and Jewish refugees, declared "war." When Russia was attacked and forced to join the allied camp, Trujillo praised Stalin, referred to Communism as "one of the great forces for welfare and progress on which the democratic world can count," and even as late as 1946 permitted a token communist faction to operate in the Dominican Republic. But when Stalin resumed the offensive and the cold war began, Trujillo was as quick to proclaim himself "the world's Number One Anti-Communist" and to use this new incarnation to persecute not only the Communists but every liberal and democratic foe of his regime who could be smeared with guilt by association.

Trujillo's one aggressive act in the field of foreign policy turned out to be his greatest blunder. The immediate cause of the massacre of

Haitians that took place in early October of 1937 is still obscure. For years the Dominican government had encouraged Haitian cane cutters to cross the border and seek seasonal employment on the (then) American-owned sugar plantations. With the fall of sugar prices in the early thirties, Haitians continued to come and many remained. There is some evidence that Trujillo, with German backing, had entered into secret negotiations with Haitian General Demosthènes Calixte for a bloodless coup that would have put the Generalissimo in control of the entire island. Whether Haiti's President Sténio Vincent was in on the negotiations is not known, but according to one version of the incident, when a photograph of Trujillo's check for $150,000 made out to Calixte appeared in a New York newspaper, Trujillo drove to Dajabón and shouted to his army chiefs, assembled in the border town, "We've been betrayed!"—adding, more or less rhetorically, "Kill every Haitian found on Dominican soil!"

The order, whatever the circumstances of its issuance, was obeyed literally. At Pedernales, Jimaní, Bánica, Dajabón, and other frontier posts, the fleeing Haitians who were not able to get across the rivers were either shot with Krag rifles and thrown to the crocodiles or penned into improvised stockades and butchered with machetes. All over the country, peasants and domestics were cut down, one unsuspecting peasant girl, the story goes, with the carving knife of her officer-master, as she served the roast. Estimates of the number massacred vary from a minimum of twelve thousand to a maximum of twenty-five thousand.

The news was suppressed by both Vincent and Trujillo, but by November it had leaked out to the foreign press, and in Washington ministers Élie Lescot of Haiti and Andrés Pastoriza of the Dominican Republic were asked by President Roosevelt to give an immediate accounting. When the truth (or part of it) was known, the terms of the Inter-American Convention signed at Gondra in 1923 were invoked. A three-nation investigating committee was named and instructed to confirm the details. But at this point, apparently, Trujillo and Vincent made a "deal" to prevent the kind of investigation that would have led to the downfall of both rulers. Trujillo paid $750,000 indemnity to Haiti, to cover the allegedly "accidental" killing of a few Haitian "interlopers," and the two presidents gave notice that they would "retire" (neither did). Vincent removed Calixte as army chief, and renamed Port-au-Prince's most important thoroughfare "Avenue Trujillo." Trujillo, for his part, proposed renaming Dajabón after Franklin D. Roosevelt—a gesture that was abandoned after horrified representations from the American Department of State.

Later, much later (1939), after installing Peynado and Troncoso in the national palace, the Dominican dictator journeyed to the United States where millions had already been spent on publicity to counteract the news of the massacre. He was received in Washington by a State Department delegation, by Secretary Hull (who was later to call Trujillo "a splendid President, who is outstanding among all those in the American nations"), and by President and Mrs. Roosevelt at the White House. Even Haiti's minister, Lescot, later to become Vincent's successor as president, got into the act by giving an official luncheon for the man who had just brought about the slaying of thousands of his countrymen. On July 12, well guarded by the Secret Service, Trujillo's private railroad car brought him to New York where he installed himself in a palatial suite at the Waldorf-Astoria. At West Point he was received by Brigadier General J. D. Benedict, the superintendent, with a twenty-one-gun salute and reviewed the cadet corps. After further receptions in New York, somewhat dampened by picket lines and the protests of liberals, Trujillo sailed for France on the *Normandie,* sending his yacht *Ramfis* ahead to meet him on the Riviera. He was cruising in the Mediterranean when Hitler invaded Poland. Quickly he took ship for home, not on the *Ramfis* which might have been accidentally torpedoed, but on an American freighter. President Roosevelt, who could easily have refused to bring him back, evidently felt, judging by subsequent events, that Trujillo would be just the man to keep the Dominican Republic in line during the years of armed struggle that lay ahead.

On May 16, 1942, Rafael Trujillo received in "free" election the combined vote of his own party, the Partido Dominicano (391,708), and of the opposition group banded together, not unsurprisingly, under the label Partido Trujillista (190,229). Thus did the dictator reassume the presidency which he was to occupy without further puppetry for the next ten years.

It would be a mistake to think that the meaning of such a pervasive phenomenon as the Trujillo dictatorship can be conveyed in terms of its economics or politics alone. The savagery, cynicism, and vulgarity of its ambience filtered from the top down, infecting the whole of Dominican society. A servile press, controlled school system, and spy apparatus without precedent in the Americas, were the instruments through which the gross vanity of the tyrant and his family, and the symbols through which they sought to perpetuate their memory, were foisted upon a terrorized and increasingly demoralized population.

The story of the press is short and unsavory. The old newspapers, close to bankruptcy in 1930, were allowed to fold, leaving the field to Trujillo's *La Nación.* An American newspaperman, Stanley Ross, sold the dictator the idea of meeting criticism abroad by establishing an "independent" competitor. This was *El Caribe,* founded in 1947, directed by the gangster Paulino from 1949 to 1954, and edited by Ross. In 1954 Germán Ornes, a liberal with a record of student rebelliousness and opposition to the regime, was permitted to buy the paper. "Due to my own weakness," wrote Ornes frankly later on, "or the strength of the adversary I eventually succumbed, as do most Dominicans living within the country and many who live abroad. I was 'broken in' and became an active collaborator. . . . I do not try to justify myself; it was a shotgun wedding, bound to end in divorce." Before the divorce came—Ornes was lucky enough to be abroad when a typographical error in a caption made reference, unpardon-ably, to Trujillo's "tomb"—*El Caribe* with half-truths and lies put up a plausible front of objectivity, while its "Public Forum" column needled the dictator's lukewarm friends prior to their disgrace.

As in all totalitarian systems, education—as an instrument of propaganda and a means of short-circuiting dangerous thoughts— thrived under Trujillo. Enrollment in the schools increased from 50,739 in 1930 to 423,424 in 1957. Hostos' educational progressivism was outlawed. One of the new primers carried the following admonition: "The President works unceasingly for the happiness of his people. . . . It is he who maintains peace [and] supports the schools. . . . If you should find in your home a man who wishes to disturb order, see that he is handed over to the police."

Every citizen was obliged to carry not only a personal identity card—without which it was impossible to travel, work, marry, drive, or vote—but a certificate of good conduct from the secret police. By 1957 there were, in addition to General Arturo Espaillat's security service, at least six other spying agencies, including the army and navy intelligences, the "Veterans" (successors to La 42), the Partido Dominicano inspectors, the palace bodyguard security, and the police, all supplying Trujillo with separate dossiers on unreliables *and on each other*. One bureau was set up only to spy on university students —especially those who had declined to work for the government. The fear of talking to anyone was summed up in the proverb: *en bocas cerradas no entran moscas.*

The dominant Catholic Church, until the final years of the regime, affected to remain outside or above politics. But acquiescence in the blasphemous *"Dios y Trujillo"* neon signs, congratulatory messages from the Pope, and the appearance of Cardinal Spellman at the dictator's jubilee, where the prelate embraced Trujillo publicly and called him "Benefactor of the Church," raised doubts about the Church's neutrality in many minds. Charges that some priests used the confessional to inform on penitents hostile to the regime are impossible to prove. There is no doubt, though, that a number of influential clerics joined the final conspiracies and that at least one was a martyr in that cause.

The extent to which a much smaller religious community, that of the Jews, was taken in by Trujillo, and collaborated in the world-wide

favorable publicity that followed the dictator's offer of a haven to
one hundred thousand refugees in 1938, is contained in this testimony
by one of their number, Bruno Phillip, Consul General of Israel in
1963:

> One hundred and sixty Jewish families remain out of the total of five
> hundred to six hundred families that came here. A somewhat larger
> number of Spanish Republicans came at the same time, but proving to
> be a political liability they were not treated well, and most of them
> re-emigrated to Mexico. Those of us who stayed prospered with our
> cheese and sausage cooperatives at Sosua. What did it all prove?
> Trujillo needed ambassadors of good will. Tired of politics and perse-
> cution abroad, we Jews complied. He used us. He used *me*. After all, he
> had done nothing but good things *for us*. Like the others I didn't
> believe in the tales of murder and corruption at first. Why, just a year
> before his death he came unannounced to a service at our synagogue.
> There he sat, gazing raptly at the Torah for two hours. After the service
> he mingled freely with us, slapping us heartily on the back and joking.
> "Can I have a visa for Israel?" he asked me. "Why not, your Excel-
> lency?" "Ah! Don't be so quick. Don't forget I'm the good friend of
> Nasser!" (roars of laughter). So he was our friend. Hadn't he given
> us $60,000 for our synagogue? So we told people how maligned he
> was by Communist propaganda. Just as the "good Germans" had kept
> their eyes closed to the extermination of our people in the Death Camps,
> which they had "never heard of," so we kept our eyes closed. We saw
> no evil. We heard no evil. We did well. We made money. Even when
> neighbors disappeared, we didn't notice—or attributed their disappear-
> ance to natural causes. We noticed nothing unusual. *We didn't want to.*
> As they say in your country, "We was had."

Foreigners, far from the hypnotic eye of *El Benefactor,* "was had."
Paulo Hasslacher, the Brazilian ambassador, Francisco del Rio
Cañedo, head of a Mexican diplomatic mission, American businessmen like William B. Pawley and John Hagen, added their voices to
the chorus of praise. Pan-American World Airways and Esso Standard took full-page ads to laud his accomplishments. And Stanley
Walker, once city editor of the New York *Herald Tribune,* wrote a
fulsome book, printed and distributed at Dominican taxpayers' ex-

pense, for the Dominican Information Center of New York. The majority of educated Dominicans yielded, in Ornes' words, to "the desire to get rich as fast as possible or to become one of the members of the small circle of favorites of the Dictator . . . even knowing that everything may be lost at the slightest whim of the Benefactor."

In this moral climate, the spectacle of Trujillo and his unseemly family began to emerge in a lurid light. The drive for self-deification, which had begun in the early thirties with the assumption of the titles "Generalissimo" and "'Benefactor of the Fatherland," the changing of the capital's name to "Ciudad Trujillo," and the replacement of the names of time-honored provinces with those of assorted ruffians-of-the-blood, now exceeded a parody of burlesque. Bronze plaques, with Trujillo's picture in color, manufactured in Mexico for $2, were forced upon every merchant in the land for $30. "Men are not indispensable," thundered *La Nación,* "but Trujillo is irreplaceable!"

The dictator's disreputable family was apparently irreplaceable too. Ramfis, the eldest son born in 1929, was commissioned a colonel at the age of four. A fourteen-year-old daughter, politely refused admittance as an "Ambassador" to the coronation of Elizabeth II, became the cause of a British minister's framing and ouster. An older daughter, after four notorious marriages, was given an official post in Washington from which to court the depraved good will of American café society. The tyrant's third wife satisfied some atavistic literary ambition by being officially proclaimed "The First Lady of Caribbean Letters" and (as if in praise) "the equal of Norman Vincent Peale," following publication of ghost-written *Moral Meditations* and a "play" which even the cringing drama critics felt willing to review only in terms of the elegant wardrobe displayed in the last act. A sister married to a chief of staff gave birth to another chief of staff. A brother made a quick fortune in Paris selling passports to desperate refugees. Another brother committed suicide after a paranoic army career and the fathering of an idiot son. A third brother waxed rich upon the control of prostitution. A fourth ran a lawsuits racket and a charcoal monopoly. A fifth hid under his mother's bed after an abortive plot against Big Brother, but finally settled down with a gambling casino, radio and television stations, and a lieutenant-generalship. A sixth, the dim-witted Hector, emerged from his vast estate *Engombe* to front for Rafael in the presidential chair.

The sign over the lunatic asylum at Nigua—"We owe everything to Trujillo"—might indicate that the dictator had suppressed the people's sense of humor along with everything else. But there was a popular saying of the time to refute this: "The brothers export, the brothers-in-law import, the head of the family deports."

And Rafael Trujillo himself, what manner of man was he? It was too late to say. If he had ever had a believable personality and a private life with human traits, creditable witnesses had long since vanished. Was he, as some said, a man who neither forgot his enemies nor forgave his friends? That covered but a part of it. Was he the very paragon of an astute capitalist? When he asked his Puerto Rican friend, the contractor Benítez Rexach, for an estimate of his expected profit on rebuilding the capital's docks and was told "$800,000," he is reported to have opened a pocket and said, "Good. I want $400,000 of that *in cash,* here, before you leave the country." Was it a little extreme, when building a hospital, to take a personal cut on the contract, the cement and steel, the bulldozers and cranes, the plumbing, the furnishings, and even the medicines? Was it quite cricket when the paint factory of one's competitor mysteriously caught fire to have the fire trucks delayed and the insurance company refuse to pay?

Was Trujillo, as his enemies insisted, a libidinous goat? Women from abroad were quick to note his "bedroom eyes" and wolfish gestures. Native mothers in the capital's society would go to extreme lengths to keep attractive daughters from official functions. His aides were observed combing the medical journals for the latest in stimulants and virility restoratives. And the only jokes about Trujillo that were allowed to pass censorship were those celebrating his supposed exploits with women. Trujillo's appetite for erotic poetry was well known, an appetite not usually present in men whose sexual impulses find normal outlets.

CATHEDRAL. Earliest and noblest of Spanish buildings in the Hemisphere, "the cathedral [in Old Santo Domingo] is built of golden, warm-glowing coral limestone, which cuts easily but weathers to diamond hardness."

COLUMBUS' TOMB. The late nineteenth-century "tomb" for Columbus defaces the entrance to the nave of the historic cathedral, was built following the discovery of the explorer's bones in a chancel crypt near the altar.

JUAN PABLO DUARTE. First and most eminent of Dominicans, the father of his country died in exile.

THREE NOBLE DOMINICAN RULERS. Ulises Espaillat (*lower left*). Second only to Duarte, this great Dominican liberal warned eloquently of tyrants to come. Ramón Cáceres (*upper left*). Ablest of constitutional rulers, the beloved "Mon" was struck down in his prime. Horacio Vásquez (*upper right*). Last and least corruptible of the Cibao's romantic horsemen, Vásquez outlived his time.

CALLE EL CONDE. Principal thoroughfare and shopping center of Santo Domingo.

CHILDREN. Blood lines combine to form the loveliest of native types.

ON THE BORDER. Between the Dominican Republic and Haiti, the pure African.

RAFAEL LEONIDAS TRUJILLO MOLINA. The Dictator wears, as always, his military finery.

"DOCTOR TRUJILLO." The Benefactor guards the entrance to the university.

PALACIO NACIONAL. First of the Dictator's architectural monuments.

EL EMBAJADOR. Largest of several luxury hotels in the Dominican capital.

LA FERIA. One of the handsome buildings at the International Fair of Peace and Brotherhood.

TYRANNICIDES. Imbert and Amiama, only survivors of Trujillo killing.

COUNCIL OF STATE. Convening in the National Palace, February, 1963.

FORTRESS. Symbol of oppression and cruelty from Columbus' time to the present, it overlooks the Ozama.

JUAN BOSCH. PRD leader and first freely-elected Dominican president since
Vásquez, Bosch was deposed by the *coup d'état* of September 25, 1963.

VIRIATO FIALLO. Leader of the first mass anti-Trujillist demonstrations and UCN presidential candidate in the December, 1962, election.

SIC TRANSIT GLORIA. Trujillo memorial at San Francisco de Macorís, one of many, as it looks today.

NATIVE ARTS. Dominicans triumphed for first time over bad taste of Trujillo era in this Episcopal church in the capital.

PEASANT HOME. Revival of indigenous culture will depend upon the city man's capacity to draw upon the country man's natural simplicity, taste, and good sense.

Inevitably—as with all criminals cowardly enough to burn the evidence—the public would have to wait upon a weighing of the most exaggerated claims pro and con to form any estimate of Trujillo's personality. Few would be satisfied with the image purveyed to the foreign press: connoisseur of art, horseman, country gentleman, man of the world. Failing to reveal his inner nature, Trujillo would have to be judged by the symbols he erected in the hope that they would reveal his ideals. In a way he never intended, they do.

Although the thirteen-foot gold-plated statue, which stood at the entrance to the largest monument ever built for a living man, was overturned and pulverized by the infuriated mobs of 1961-62, the monument itself—inhuman, funerary, preposterous—continues to dominate the Cibao like a petrified phallus.

The International Fair of 1955-56, dedicated like the Santiago monument to "Peace" and "Brotherhood," took tangible shape in a complex of seventy-nine buildings, a complete Coney Island imported from the United States, and a tawdry million-dollar fountain of music and light. Expected to bring in five hundred thousand tourists, the fair attracted twenty-four thousand, many of them flown in, expenses paid, as part of an enormous publicity campaign to counteract the increasingly ugly image of Trujillismo abroad. The fair's symbolism was best revealed in two "Golden Albums" of morroco-bound rotogravure, frontispieced by a tinted portrait of the Dictator in gold braid, and largely devoted to the rites attendant upon the coronation of "Her Gracious Majesty Angelita I," Trujillo's youngest daughter. In her eighty-thousand dollar Italian gown, diamond-studded tiara, and ponytail (which reportedly cost a thousand dollars to invert), the "precious" queen is pictured a hundred times, passing through the orgies of ribbon cutting, speech making, champagne swilling, and pig kissing, while her father, in several dozen of his thousand suits and uniforms, greets the few foreign dignitaries—President Kubitschek of Brazil, the special envoy of Generalissimo Franco, Cardinal Spellman, and the ambassadors of Cuba, Venezuela, and the United States—who could be lured into fawning upon his apotheosis.

About this time the Dictator, perhaps as a sop to his third wife, María Martínez, who was constantly imploring him to escape to Europe with their loot before too late, bought the world's largest diesel-powered sailing vessel and christened it *Angelita.* A more modest excursion vessel (the 250-foot frigate *Benefactor*) had fared badly when the addition of a swimming pool had flooded the decks and her stacks had set fire to the huge mahogany bar. *Angelita,* with her thirty-four thousand square feet of sail, air conditioning and tele-vision, radar, sonar, automatic pilot, gyroscopic compass, refrigeration plants, and mechanical horse (to keep Angelita's weight down), was better suited to the family's needs. Once it carried the fun-loving group on a vacation jaunt to Acapulco and Los Angeles via the Canal. Today, heavily guarded and at considerable cost, it lies in the Ozama boat basin, a copy of the latest book on polo at Ramfis' bedside table, and in the Generalissimo's closet a framed facsimile of the American Declaration of Independence in petit point.

Near the gateway to his estate *Fundación*—by 1960 proliferating from its original three thousand acres into adjoining provinces and guarded at checkpoints along the wall by machine gun nests—Tru-jillo built an "informal" home, calling it after his favorite wood *La Caoba.* Here, too, everything remains as it was: the closets with row on row of uniforms made to order in Washington; the racks of hundred-dollar painted neckties; the tricolored sashes and jeweled identification bracelets; the pottery ashtrays molded to resemble catcher's mitts and crooked meerschaums; the wine decanters blown into grape clusters; the American calendars ("Fine Cattle Produce Fine Milk"); the cheap chromo snow scene behind the desk with its legend, "Christ Is Supreme in This House"; the private bedroom carpeted two inches deep with the Dominican flag, its bed so arranged that his companion would have to be watching the Virgin and Child. . . .

It was toward this bed and its latest occupant that the old lecher, his crimes about to catch up with him, was driving lightheartedly on the fateful evening of May 30, 1961.

X

Liberation and Upheaval, 1960-63

From the Assassination of Trujillo
to the Overthrow of Juan Bosch

Whatever else Rafael Leonidas Trujillo Molina was thinking of that night of May 30, 1961, as his unescorted Chevrolet sped along the Avenida Jorge Washington, through the International Fair of Peace and Brotherhood, and out onto the four-lane *autopista* leading to San Cristobal where his twenty-year-old mistress, Moni Sánchez, lay waiting for him, he was not thinking of the ingenuity of those who had tried to waylay him in the past. Not one of them had come close to succeeding.

The first serious conspiracy, a naval invasion launched from Cayo Confites during the summer of 1947, never got beyond Cuban territorial waters. A group of students in Havana University, inspired by the precedent of Máximo Gomez, the Dominican general who had helped José Martí liberate Cuba from the tyranny of Spain, met secretly. Among the Dominicans was Angel Miolán, later to become Juan Bosch's party chief. Among the Cubans was Fidel Castro. A wealthy Dominican exile, General Juancito Rodriguez, provided funds. The conspiracy was at least tolerated by President Grau San Martín until one of Trujillo's agents in Cuba got to Grau and hinted that the expedition, if successful, would return to "liberate" Cuba. Then the Cuban Navy intervened and it was all over.

Two years later, backed by Guatemala's president, Juan Arévalo, and captained by Horacio Ornes (brother of *El Caribe's* owner-editor, Germán), a single PBY flying boat with fourteen aboard managed to land off the north Dominican coast and seize the village of Luperón. Four of the invaders were captured and later permitted to go abroad—Trujillo hoped that they would testify to the "Communist" support for the invasion; the others were hunted down and killed in the mountains. Trujillo seems to have known the details of this plot well in advance.

His secret police were also well alerted to the next attempt, a 1956 conspiracy to assassinate Trujillo in the same place that had witnessed Heureaux's exit, Moca. Its failure received nothing like the publicity attendant upon the March 12, 1956, kidnaping in New York of Jesús María de Galíndez. Galíndez was a Basque scholar and soldier in the army of Loyalist Spain who had lived in the Dominican Republic from 1937 to 1946. In New York he had been engaged in preparing a doctoral thesis (subsequently published in Chile as *La Era de Trujillo*) on the dictatorship. Although the secret police files were destroyed by the Trujillo family in 1961, there is good evidence that Galíndez was spirited aboard a private plane piloted by Gerald Lester Murphy, an American employee of the Compañía Dominicana de Aviación, and flown to Monte Cristi.* Murphy was seized by the secret police (S.I.M.) and the following year was found hanging, allegedly a "suicide," in a Dominican prison. Many Dominicans believe that Trujillo personally strangled the frail professor when he was dragged before the dictator's desk in the Palacio Nacional.

* Masterminding of the American end of the kidnaping has generally been attributed to Trujillo's security chief, Arturo Espaillat, although General Espaillat did not arrive in New York to take over as consul general until some weeks after the actual crime. In his sketchy account of service with Trujillo (*Trujillo: The Last of the Caesars*), Espaillat—on no other evidence than a column by Drew Pearson—charges that Galindez had received more than a million dollars from the Central Intelligence Agency to overthrow Generalissimo Franco of Spain, and he implies that only the CIA can now solve the mystery of the kidnaping.

Details of what happened in the invasion attempt of June 14, 1959, jointly backed by President Betancourt of Venezuela and Premier Castro of Cuba in the days before they became bitter enemies, are elusive. Landings by boat took place at Maimon and at Estero Hondo; by plane at Constanza. The returning exiles were either betrayed to Trujillo in advance or tragically overestimated the anticipated native support. Dominicans insist that the United States quickly drew a naval cordon around the island to prevent reinforcement. The invaders at Constanza were captured and tortured to death under Air Force Commander Ramfis Trujillo's personal supervision at the San Isidro air base outside the capital.

In February of 1960 President Betancourt asked the Organization of American States to censure Trujillo for "flagrant violations of human rights." He had good reasons. In June of that year Betancourt had narrowly escaped death from a dynamite bomb in Caracas; investigation of the triggering device showed it to have been made in the Dominican Republic. The OAS responded to this effort to export Trujillismo in naked form by calling a meeting of the hemisphere's foreign ministers at San José, Costa Rica. The ministers voted unanimously for economic sanctions and called on all American nations, including the United States, to break diplomatic relations with Trujillo. This was done.

Trujillo's position was not desperate, but he began to act as though it were. The treasury, already in arrears from the multimillion-dollar "Fair" fiasco, was further depleted by a panicky cash purchase of additional jet fighter planes. A small-arms plant, first disguised as a zipper factory, went into full production, although only Ramfis' elite three-thousand-man air force was issued more than a few rounds of ammunition. What hurt most was the loss of $30,000,000 in sugar sales that followed the punitive excise tax imposed by President Eisenhower on the Dominican quota which a generous Congress had raised from 27,000 tons to 250,000 tons following Fidel Castro's switch to the Communist bloc. This, with the diversion of all international exchange funds into the family accounts abroad, the assumption by the Dictator of the presidency of the Dominican Central Bank, and a decree ordering that all exporters deposit 90 per cent of their dollar earnings with him, shook the business community out of its thirty-year-old funk.

In January of 1960 the Catholic Church, sensing the dictatorship's impending fall, issued a pastoral letter denouncing the erstwhile friend and benefactor upon whom it had once conferred its highest decoration. And Trujillo, for his part, retaliated with radio broadcasts accusing "reactionary" priests and nuns of the grossest immoralities. Two bishops, Riley in San Juan and Panal in La Vega, risked their lives by making common cause with the underground. One of them, in fact, was charged with complicity in the latest assassination attempt—a January 21, 1960, mining of the Cattle Coliseum at the fairgrounds that missed detonation with El Jefe aboard by just five hours. Only the confusion of the bigger roundup that followed the climactic act of May 30 saved Riley. The coldblooded murder in 1960 of the Mirabel sisters for spurning El Jefe's advances aroused widespread indignation. Screams of other victims, on the amplifying system deliberately hooked up to the cell blocks at the S.I.M.'s torture house *La Cuarenta* and the air force's "Kilometer Nine" outside the city, began to echo throughout the nation.

With the leftist and idealistic youth undergrounds decimated and under control, membership in the two small groups that now met to take effective direct action was pretty much restricted to disgruntled business and military leaders who had lost power. Luis Amiama Tió, a former mayor of Santo Domingo (then Ciudad Trujillo) who had extensive banana and transportation interests, was one. Antonio de la Maza, an army officer and lumber magnate who had had a brother killed by the dictator, was another. Antonio Imbert Barrera, an ex-governor of Puerto Plata Province, was a third. Brigadier General Juan Tomás Diaz, forced into premature retirement by Trujillo in 1960, was a fourth. Contacts with the American consulate were established, and the Central Intelligence Agency (CIA) entered the picture, smuggling in three M-1 rifles of World War II vintage with five hundred rounds of ammunition. These weapons, disassembled, were shipped in marked food cans to Lorenzo Berry, American operator of "Wimpy's" supermarket in a fashionable district, who in turn passed them along to an American appliances dealer, Tom Stocker, who kept them in a closet in his home until May 27. On that day they were picked up by one of the Dominican conspirators. Following the dismal failure of the CIA-organized "Bay of Pigs" invasion in April, orders were issued to postpone the killing, lest the United States be embarrassed by a second failure, but it was too late.

The conspiracy, which now included many generals in its membership, called for one of them, José René Román Fernández, secretary of state for the armed forces and Trujillo's nephew-in-law, to receive the body of the slain dictator, broadcast the news of their liberation to the people, and summon the members of the "Royal Family" to the Ozama Fortress where they would be killed. Everything but the actual assassination was bungled..

At 10:30 on the moonlit night of May 30, two carloads of armed men intercepted the dictator's unescorted vehicle just beyond La Feria Ganadera. Trujillo's chauffeur was winged but escaped. Trujillo himself jumped out, fired a few shots from his automatic, but went down with twenty-seven bullets in him. Dumping the body into the trunk of one of the cars, the conspirators drove to Juan Tomás Díaz' house. They then looked for General Román, only to find that Trujillo had earlier ordered him to go to the San Isidro base and stay there. In panic, the conspirators abandoned the car. Instead of dispatching Pedro Livio Cedeño, who had been wounded by one of Trujillo's shots (Imbert was slightly wounded by another), they took him to a private clinic while four others hid in the home of Dr. Robert Reid Cabral. The S.I.M., alerted, closed in. The doctor and his patient were both put to torture, and the patient talked. Antonio de la Maza, who had fired the fatal shots, was gunned down in the street, together with Díaz. Even the tapes, that had been prerecorded to broadcast the good news, were captured intact. Only Imbert and Amiama were able to escape into hiding. General Román was taken to "Kilometer Nine," where he was left for days with his eyelids stitched to his eyebrows, beaten with baseball bats, drenched with acid, exposed to swarms of angry ants, castrated, and shocked for hours on end in the electric chair; fifty-six machine gun slugs finally put him out of his misery.

On May 31, Ramfis, who had been playing polo in Paris with his former brother-in-law, Porfirio Rubiroso, chartered a $27,000 private flight and flew home to supervise this operation. On June 1, unable to suppress the news longer, *El Caribe* appeared with the following headlines:

VILMENTE ASESINEDO CAE EL
BENEFACTOR DE LA PATRIA

SU MUERTE LLENA DE LUTO
LA SOCIEDAD DOMINICANA

And under this a eulogistic obituary by the newly-named president, Joaquin Balaguer, concluded: *"Por Trujillo y por la Patria, pido a todos la colaboración y la conducta austera de que debemos dar prueba en esta hora suprema de dolor."* A poem of mourning consolation that appeared in the paper several days later, however, was found to contain a more truthful message; alert readers discovered that the first letter of each line, read from top to bottom, spelled "Asesino y Ladrón."

For a few days the bloodbath continued unabated. The United States, though it continued to keep all anti-Trujillo Dominicans from entering the country, intervened to the extent of giving some protection to Americans involved in the plot. But on June 11 an OAS committee arrived and served notice on the degenerate Ramfis that the reign of terror must end. Ramfis' authority was to be confined henceforth to the armed forces, and he was advised that if he restrained himself he could leave the country a rich man. Balaguer was given more power, but Hector and Arismendi Trujillo, "the wicked uncles," moved in to see that he exercised it in their behalf.

For six months this uneasy state of affairs was permitted to continue, with the Trujillo family completing its expropriation of what remained of the country's movable wealth. All incriminating police records were destroyed, and preparations were made for a quick escape if "conditions deteriorated." Meanwhile, the Kennedy administration in Washington was trying to come up with a new Latin American policy—a policy that would permit "intervention" again, but this time in behalf of democratic elements struggling against minority dictatorships.

As early as July the first opportunity to try out this new policy had materialized. Student rallies at the university were the first sign of reviving spirits; a leader in one of these demonstrations received mild treatment—deportation—as the Trujillos temporized to gain time, and perhaps a relaxation of the American economic squeeze. Conservative anti-Trujillo elements, under the leadership of Viriato Fiallo, were permitted to organize a National Civic Union (UCN), and on July 29 Dr. Fiallo addressed eight thousand men, women, and children in Independence Square and boldly demanded an end "to the political power, the economic power, the military power of the Trujillos." On the same day Manuel Tavares Justo, leader of leftist "14 June" movement, was released from nineteen months in the S.I.M.'s torture chambers.

On October 17 rioting students erupted into the capital's streets and a general strike began. Shopkeepers locked their shutters and went home. Many were subjected to beatings, but the strike continued. Sewer lids, with the hated dictator's name on them, were ripped from the streets, broken, and flung at the police from the roof tops. Gasoline bombs were exploded. Finally riot squads moved in with blazing guns and brought the riots to a temporary halt. But Ramfis, beginning to bend under the American pressure now exerted constantly, agreed to send the two brothers abroad and in return received a promise of the termination of the boycott.

This truce was short-lived. By mid-November, although Ramfis had flown back to Paris where most of his millions were secured, Hector and Arismendi Trujillo were still in power. In fact they were now rallying the army and secret police for a "final solution," in which every known enemy of Trujillismo at home and abroad was to be slain.

Two events forestalled this massacre. Pedro Rodríguez Echavarria, the air force commander in Santiago, became a national hero overnight by rounding up most of the available warplanes, winning the support of the army, and forcing the brothers to leave the country again. His task was made easier by the sudden appearance of fourteen American warships, including two aircraft carriers, just outside the three-mile limit off Santo Domingo. Three squadrons of American fighter jets at the same time roared over the waterfront—and were cheered by the Dominicans. Balaguer "rewarded" Echavarria by making him secretary of state for the armed forces. Balaguer was indeed trying desperately to hang on now. He was handing out favors right and left—especially left. He was posing as a liberal, a friend of labor, a revolutionary-at-heart, but his thirty-year record as a rubber stamp for Trujillo, and especially his cowardice before the United Nations in New York in October—when he might have denounced Ramfis and the brothers and brought them down, but instead said not a word in their disfavor—could not be forgotten. In December, Balaguer permitted the moderate opposition to participate in the government by way of a council of state which would have legislative and limited executive powers. Its members, in addition to Balaguer himself as president, were: Rafael F. Bonelly, a former Trujillo cabinet member and ambassador who had now joined the UCN, vice president; Dr. Nicholas Pichardo, second vice president; Eliseo Perez Sánchez, archbishop of Santo Domingo; Eduardo Read Barreras;* and, as a sop to the public, the two surviving tyrannicides, Amiama and Imbert, both of whom were later commissioned brigadier generals.

* Later replaced by Dr. José A. Fernández Caminero.

Wild jubilation ensued. All over the country the last of the Trujillo statues and street signs were ripped down. The university, closed since October, reopened, and its campus was declared "inviolate" territory. The name of the capital was restored to Santo Domingo. Exiles began to return by the planeload from all over Latin America.

As January, 1962, moved into its final weeks, the position of the real rulers, Balaguer and Echavarria, became intolerable. The "wicked uncles" were known to be hovering offshore again—would they return? The UCN was mounting loudspeakers in the *Parque Independencia* and broadcasting provocations to the people to stage an effective uprising—provocations that any strong government would have treated as seditious, but that Balaguer's, without popular support, hesitated to suppress. General Echavarria, now reverting to type, did not hesitate. On January 16 tanks were ordered into the city. Machine guns opened up on the crowd outside UCN headquarters, killing six and wounding a score. That night Echavarria seized the members of the council—save Amiama and Imbert, who "joined" his junta until they could hide in the American embassy— and rushed them to San Isidro.

Echavarria's *coup d'état* lasted exactly forty-eight hours. Driving to San Isidro, the United States Chargé d'Affaires John Calvin Hill served notice on the would-be Napoleon that his XVIIIth Brumaire was over. The "Junta" would not be recognized, promised economic aid would be canceled, the $55,000,000 sugar quota would go elsewhere, the fleet (just over the horizon) might resume its menacing patrol of the waterfront at any moment. The capital, he did not need to add, was already in the grip of a second and more effective general strike. The army—it was still the old Trujillo army, after all —now realized that nothing but capitulation to the popular mood could save it. Under mob rule—with Communism the certain ultimate victor—or American intervention, it would be liquidated. It acted upon this sobering thought without further ado. Echavarria was arrested with his closest air force associates, and together with

Balaguer, who had prudently taken refuge in the Papal Nuncio's residence, was shipped to Puerto Rico. The council of state reconvened, with Bonelly as provisional president and Donald Reid Cabral, brother of the physician-martyr of May 30, 1961, filling Balaguer's vacated slot. It was agreed that the council would act as a caretaker-government, serving only until a free election in December, and participating in that election not at all.

During the prolonged electioneering that dominated its eleven-month tenure, the reconstituted council was charged lustily with everything from coddling capital and taking orders from the Americans to pocketing the entire $25,000,000 emergency foreign aid and laying the groundwork for new dictatorship. Inevitably, considering the broad divergence of interests among the seven councillors, there was some truth in all four charges. On the whole, however, the council did a good job and carried out its major objective scrupulously.

Cynics who believed the worst of the rumors that the councillors were feathering their own nests and had not completed any of the new schools they were supposed to be building, would not concede that the free election had been a council triumph. In their dark view, the majority of councillors favoring a Fiallo victory had simply been caught off base by the sudden swing to Bosch in the final week—and had been prevented from rigging the count only by the presence of OAS observers and the proximity of the American fleet. The best answer to the second charge was that the election *had* been carried out without incident, and that the party of the underdogs, opposed by the governing group, *had won*. An answer to the first was the unprecedented prosperity. "Wimpy's" supermarket, which had never employed more than sixteen people under Trujillo, was employing forty in December of 1962. Wages and salaries were double or more what they had been two years before. People had money to spend, and whole planeloads of middle-class folk were flying to Puerto Rico

with their families for the day, just to buy shoes or to see the forbidden outside world. With the *pesos* generated by the $25,000,000
loan, the council financed most of the A.I.D. program (including
CARE, with its hot lunches for ninety-one thousand school children
in the impoverished northwest), introduced a new and badly needed
first grade reader, built or commenced building thirteen new schools,
made loans to the housing bank, and put through some agrarian
reform including several model institutes at which *campesinos* were
given instruction in modern growing methods and cooperative self-
help.*

There were irregularities and some graft, inevitably, and Juan
Bosch's militant Partido Revolucionario Dominicano (PRD) concentrated its attack on the right wing of the council, Archbishop
Perez and Antonio Imbert in particular, and charged that Manuel
Imbert's cement trust and the American Esso Standard company were
receiving favors. Caminero and Pichardo were considered to be
furthest "left" among the councillors, and the latter the ablest. But
Donald Reid, although frequently sick, overworked, and distracted,
gave the council a badly needed moral tone. Independently wealthy,
this frail, courageous young man helped most to give the council the
public respect that enabled it to survive the barrage of criticism.

Since the election campaign quickly narrowed down to a contest
between Viriato Fiallo and Juan Bosch and was determined as much
by the personalities of these two leaders as by the programs of their
parties, it may be helpful to review their backgrounds.

Fiallo, as we have already seen, had become the acknowledged
leader of the anti-Trujillist urban masses in the months following the
dictator's death. A nephew of General Federico Fiallo, Trujillo's

---

* In this last, as well as in a wide variety of technical jobs, and above all by giving
proof that idealistic young Americans were ready to live at the level of poorer Dominicans while helping them, the Peace Corps did more than any American group to establish better Dominican-American relations.

chief of staff in the forties, Dr. Fiallo had managed to pursue his career as a respected physician throughout the Trujillo era without compromising himself. He had been several times imprisoned, once spending thirty days in a cell so small he had to crouch on his knees. No intellectual, and without political experience, Fiallo soon became surrounded by advisors who played upon his simple-minded faith that if every trace of the old order and every individual who had worked for Trujillo were eliminated from the public scene, the Republic's problems would be solved. This policy—or lack of a policy—expressed in the good doctor's often reiterated phrase *"Basta ya!"* pleased the *turbas* in the days of street rioting, but in the campaign it tended to alienate not only the civil servants and soldiers, but the masses as well. The former, quite naturally, were apprehensive about a purge that might eliminate all who had even been seen shaking hands with El Jefe. The latter wanted more of a radical land reform program than Fiallo and his conservative business friends were ready to offer. The sunglasses the portly doctor wore, so reminiscent of the standard garb of Trujillo's henchmen, did not help him. And the campaign carried on in *Union Civica,* the paper Fiallo had founded on August 16, 1961, was inept. The last issue, printed on December 20, 1962, election day, bore the headline "BOSCH SAYS TRUJILLO KNEW HOW TO GOVERN!"; and below it a smeared photograph purported to be Check No. 115,207 for one *peso*—the implication being that Bosch had already bought that many votes, when everyone knew that the big money was behind the UCN and that the PRD could not even afford a newspaper of its own.

Juan Bosch, who had returned from twenty-six years of exile in January of 1962, was fifty-three years old. Outwardly he was everything that a statesman of a new order should be. Tall, handsomely proportioned, with craggy features and searching blue eyes, white haired and eloquent, his presence was commanding. It was thought by his well-wishers that so much intelligence, honesty, and good will would more than compensate for administrative inexperience, a measure of intellectual arrogance, and excessive vanity. Some thought

Bosch would be handicapped in his campaign by the long absence, but this turned out to be an asset. For one thing, he and his close associates could not be charged with playing it safe; nor could they be motivated by mere vengefulness against underlings of the dictatorship whose very faces they were now seeing for the first time. Bosch's entire adult life had been spent keeping the spirit of resistance alive among the exiles, gaining support for their activities among countries and individuals hostile to the tyrant, raising funds, writing editorials and manifestos. As secretary to Cuban President Prío Socorrás in the forties, he had learned something of the political futility of trying to please everyone. Later, as director of the Inter-American Institute for Political Education at San José, Costa Rica, he had recognized the possibility—indeed the necessity—of carrying out a social-agrarian revolution by democratic, non-Communist means. Somewhere in the months or weeks of relaxation between these activist pursuits, Bosch had found time to write and publish several books. And friendships with men like Betancourt, Figueres, Haya de la Torre, and Norman Thomas had confirmed his moderate socialist philosophy.

Bosch's Partido Revolucionario Dominicano, one of many combative little exile groups abroad, quickly took root and flourished in native soil. Under the driving organizational lash of Angel Miolán, it brought 100,000 peasants into a loose cooperative union and signed up 170,000 others, most of whom were too poor to pay dues, as party members. Neither the PRD nor the UCN had much to say on the foreign policy issues—Haiti, the United States, Castro. There is no denying however, that the Cuban social revolution exerted a dominant attraction over such leftist movements as the "14 June," and that in the contest to win their vote the UCN and the PRD were vying with each other. Superficially, the UCN sounded the more radical: it promised a more sweeping purge of the Trujillistas; it opposed the PRD's offer of a ten- to twenty-year tax exemption for foreign capital. But this radicalism meant little to the impoverished, land-hungry peasant. To him (and he made up the majority of voters), Fiallo's party speakers looked and talked like the city gentry Bosch was flaying mercilessly as the *tutumpotes* (big shots), with their long cars, fat wives, or sleek mistresses, crowding over the roulette tables at Trujillo's streamlined hotels, the Jaragua and the Embajador, or in sunglasses at poolside making nefarious "deals" with American capitalists. Fiallo could talk to the point of exhaustion about Bosch's "hypocrisy" in promising the landless fourteen acres each of the 70 per cent untilled acreage in the country, but this was what the peasant wanted to hear. PRD spokesmen, moreover, had this ready riposte: were not the two million acres of Trujillo estates already in the state's possession, ready to be distributed? And should this prove insufficient, by what right did the absentee landlords keep 36 per cent of all remaining arable lands untilled and fallow? These lands, Bosch insisted, must be cultivated. The unemployed city folk must be given jobs. "Take UCN's money," he shouted dramatically to cheering crowds, "and then vote for PRD!" In Santiago, heart of the rich Cibao, everyone knew on election eve that the UCN would win a majority of better than two to one; only domestics were heard muttering the popular jingle:

> Si te encuentras con Dios
> Abrázalo—es Juan Bosch.
> Si te encuentros con un gato
> Mátalo—es Viriato!

Not only was the UCN losing the peasantry, however; it was losing a substantial fraction of the middle and upper classes as well. If the burghers were apprehensive about Fiallo's promised house-cleaning, the fear of the army officers and their families can be imagined. Many believe that had Balaguer remained in the country and campaigned for himself, as he had planned to do, he would have carried the capital. As it was, Bosch carried it—thanks to Fiallo, who had driven Balaguer out. Nevertheless, a week before the election few pollsters would have given the PRD more than a fighting chance. The big break came when a young Jesuit priest named

Laútico García accused Bosch of being a "Marxist-Leninist." The Catholic Church, though certainly favoring Fiallo's candidacy, had up to that moment maintained a neutral stance; the rumor that excommunication was in store for those who voted PRD had no foundation. But the maverick priest's ill-timed charge was handled by Bosch with devastating effect. First he dramatically "withdrew" from the race. This was more than Fiallo had bargained for and aroused a storm of indignation against both the UCN and the Church. The young priest was hurriedly induced to meet Bosch in debate, on television, and to retract his charge. Bosch, a skillful debater, made a fool of him before the nation. "Our people do not like aggressive men," he said later. "They like underdogs. In the case of the Church, I was the underdog."

He was right. Thousands changed their allegiance overnight. Of the 1,200,000 eligible voters, almost a million went to the polls on December 20, 1962, and more than 600,000 voted for Bosch. Fiallo received 250,000 votes, and the parties of the more extreme left and right about 100,000 combined.

The utter rout of the UCN—it elected only three members to the twenty-four-man senate and less than a majority to the house—and its collapse as an effective movement following defeat, posed one of the problems the new President would have to face. Would the Republic become again, in effect, a one-party system, without responsible criticism to curb the natural tendency of power to fill a vacuum? Or, conversely, would the new government become immobilized in the cross fire of charges from Juan Isidro Jiménez Grullón's Alianza Social Democrata (ASD) on the right and the "14 June" on the left? Extremists monopolized the air waves as soon as the polls were closed.

Another dilemma which confronted the new administration was: how to get the *latifundia,* the big estates of the absentee landlords and of the Trujillos, distributed and back in production. Should they be parceled out to private hands or managed, as the sugar trust was already being managed, by the state? Even were this problem solved, could the landless Dominican, habituated for centuries to the Hispanic pattern of working no more than minimal need required, be induced to work? Dominican officialdom continued to honor the twenty-five-hour work week. Could the top-heavy bureaucracy, with its fantastically high salaries, and the Trujillista armed services be trimmed without inviting revolt? Wages in the sugar industry, which had jumped from $1.00 to $3.75 since Trujillo, were already pricing Dominican sugar out of competition in the world market. Could the Negro majority be educated up to taking a proportionate share in the national government (there had not been even a mulatto among the seven councillors of state, yet less than 15 per cent of the 3,100,000 Dominicans could be classified as "White")?* Above all, could the tiny economic ruling class be induced to tolerate a party, however freely elected, which threatened its traditional prerogatives; or would it, in the time-dishonored tradition, make common cause with the authoritarian "rightness" of cross and sword?

In his inaugural address of February 27, 1963, Juan Bosch gave noble expression to the hopes of most of his sorely tried compatriots:

> Let no one expect the use of hate while we are governing. We are here with the decision to work not to hate, disposed to create not to destroy, to defend and to shelter, not to persecute. Let us join our hearts together in the task of doing away with hate among Dominicans as one does away with weeds in the field to be sown. Let us join our hearts together in the task of building institutions that will give shelter to those who never had it, that will give work to those who seek without having found it, that will give land to those farmers who need it, and security not only to those born here but to all those who wander the earth in search of refuge from misery and persecution. . . .
> While we govern, liberty will not perish in the Dominican Republic.

In the seven months that Juan Bosch survived, how many of these promises were kept? There is no question that liberty flourished, as

---

* The question was not raised. Racial imbalance has never been an issue in the Dominican Republic. Yet it could easily become one.

never before. In fact those who overthrew Bosch justified their action
in large part on the grounds that complete freedom of speech, press,
assemblage, and travel had permitted Castro-Communists to infil-
trate the body politic to the critical point. Even Bosch's friends had
become alarmed by the extent to which demagogues of the left and
right were monopolizing the channels of propaganda. Bosch's answer
to the criticism that he was being "soft on Communism" was that he
could observe the Communists better while they were in the open,
and that he had been elected to safeguard freedom of expression for
all. Nevertheless, permitting thirty Castro sympathizers to go to
Cuba for the July 26 jamboree there, when Dominican passports
expressly prohibited travel to Russia and its satellites, was viewed
as exceeding impartiality—especially when this had followed directly upon a meeting with military officers in which the President
had been urged to adopt a clear-cut anti-Communist line. The
President's refusal to do so, and his subsequent dismissal of an air
force chaplain on unproved charges of complicity in the officers'
demands, made a showdown inevitable. And upon whom could
Bosch rely in a showdown? It was shortly after this that Germán
Ornes, whose *El Caribe* had been tolerant to Bosch during and after
the election, wrote: "Bosch is alienating everybody one by one—the
press, the church, business, and even people who were his most enthusiastic supporters, political liberals."

But if Bosch could be excused for excessive zeal in this area—he
did, after all, keep his promise to protect the freedoms, and there
was no violence while he remained in office—the answer to whether
he gave the Republic good government, and the disinherited majority
a stake in the economic potential, had to be "No." Apologists insisted that men of ability, especially businessmen and political opponents, had refused to cooperate with the new governmment; and that
in seven months there was neither the time nor the cash resources to
resettle the landless on the available Trujillo lands. But although
there is much truth in both arguments, the fact that the administration was staffed with incompetents, and that when President Bosch
was unceremoniously seized, the huge majority that had jubilantly

voted him in stood by in complete indifference, cannot be overlooked. Like so many Latin American moderate socialists before him, Bosch's will to radically reform his country became paralyzed by his fear that in wholeheartedly accepting American aid he would be accused of compromising Dominican sovereignty.

No matter how tragic were the failures of Bosch and his party, nothing that was done (or not done) could justify the *coup d'état* of September 25, 1963. It was not an uprising of the people, it came in response to no popular demand, it could not even be said to represent the will of Juan Bosch's political and business foes. It was the unprincipled act of a small clique of military men, holdovers psychologically and in fact from the thirty-two years of gangster government. Its instant, bloodless, wholly unopposed "success" attested primarily to the depth of that Hispanic malady of authoritarianism which nothing but a generation of education in democracy and a complete eradication of military autonomy could eliminate.

It could be argued that had the United States "guaranteed"— following the failure of the OAS to do so—the tenure in office of whichever party had won the free election of December, 1962, the coup could not have succeeded. The threat of American military action had, after all, prevented the return of the Trujillos. But in April of 1963, when the United States—despite a strong commitment to get rid of the corrupt Duvalier dictatorship in Haiti—had restrained the liberating Dominican forces poised on the border, it was clear that Bosch would be left to survive on his own. The rationale behind American inaction in September, 1963, not to mention acquiescence in the overthrow the same and preceding year of the constitutional governments of Guatemala, Ecuador, Peru, and Honduras, was that even benevolent intervention would be resented and ultimately prove more injurious than the evil it was designed to prevent. Perhaps. But meanwhile self-government was snuffed out before it had a chance even to be tried.

One of the many ironies of the *coup d'état* of September 25 was that Juan Bosch became the victim of the very fear that had insured his election. Fiallo in the autumn of 1962 had borne down too hard on beneficiaries of the Trujillo dictatorship. A year later, when business became apprehensive that the new government would implement its own promises of retribution, the military took advantage of that fear. Colonel Elias Wessin y Wessin instigated the coup when Bosch asked for his resignation, but if Bosch's armed forces minister, Major General Victor Elby Viñas Román, and the two tyrannicides, Generals Imbert and Amiama, had not concurred, nothing would have come of it. And if the six rightist opposition parties had not been ready to cooperate, the military might not have acted. As it was, the prompt withdrawal of American diplomatic recognition and economic aid forced the military to retire behind a civilian screen. Three distinguished conservatives—Manuel Tavares Espaillat, Ramón Tapia Espinal, and Emilio de los Santos—accepted membership in a civilian junta the day following the coup. Their feeling, and that of a cabinet that was sworn in on September 27, was presumably expressed by the new foreign minister, Donald Reid Cabral, when he called the coup "a disaster" and said that it was precisely in the hope of "avoiding the continuation of military domination" that he was participating in the new government.

Shortly before the end of 1963, the United States, though still withholding economic aid, felt obliged to recognize the junta. Failure of the conservatives to rally any popular support threatened to give the leadership of the now leaderless masses to the "14 June"—a default from which only Castro stood to gain. The death of Manuel Tavares Justo in a guerilla ambush in December merely postponed such a confrontation. An internal power struggle between Wessin y Wessin's regular army group and General Imbert, who controlled the police, threatened further instability. But could a new election—presumably the price of American recognition—promise a popular government with any greater likelihood of survival than the last?

An affirmative answer would now seem to depend on a resolution of the dilemma of American foreign policy. Benevolent "neutrality"—a high-minded unwillingness to come to the defense of a popularly-elected government that promised essential social reforms when it was threatened by a tiny military oligarchy—had resulted in disaster. When the American ambassador, John Bartlow Martin, had warned the conservative-military clique in July not to attempt a *coup d'état*, it was clear that his warning was backed up by no promise of force from Washington. The clique could, and did, act with impunity. The Alliance for Progress, for all its idealism and its millions, once again foundered because the American government itself had found no way of combating the bogus "anticommunism" the vested interests in Latin America consistently use to block that redistribution of wealth without which leftist dictatorship, imposed from abroad, is bound to triumph.

On the resolution of that dilemma, or on its evasion, the next phase of the Dominicans' five-centuries' struggle for self-determination will depend.

Appendix

Quisqueya: A Physical Description

Topography. Occupying the eastern two thirds (18,045 square miles) of the 28,249 square mile island of Hispaniola, midway between Puerto Rico and Cuba, the Dominican Republic is bounded on the north by the Atlantic Ocean, on the south by the Caribbean Sea, and on the west by the Republic of Haiti. Its eastern tip is fifty-four miles from Puerto Rico. From that tip (Cape Engaño) westward to the Haitian frontier, the distance is 260 miles. The greatest *width* (Monte Cristi in the northwest to Cape Beata in the southwest) is 170 miles. The approximate length of the Republic's coastline is 940 miles.

The two best natural harbors in the Dominican Republic are Manzanillo Bay, at the northwest Haitian border, and Samaná Bay, protected by the long Samaná Peninsula on the northeast coast. Samaná Bay, with great depth, room enough for all the ships in the world, and a defensible channel entrance only two thousand yards wide, would make the best fleet base in the West Indies—a circumstance (our history shows) that has probably kept it from being developed. Between these great and largely neglected harbors are the two principal Atlantic ports: Puerto Plata, connected by road and railway (no longer operational) with Santiago, the nation's second city; and Monte Cristi, not far from Manzanillo, at the mouth of the largest Dominican river, the Yaque del Norte. Monte Cristi, its anchorage a mile offshore, and sheltered on the east by the famous isolated butte, El Morro, is more picturesque than serviceable. Puerto

Plata has a small bay protected by a coral reef, but the channel to it is dangerous and there is not room enough inside for more than three or four freighters. There are five good harbors on the Caribbean coast: La Romana, San Pedro de Macoris, Santo Domingo, Haina, and Barahona.

There are many excellent beaches in the Dominican Republic, none of them as yet developed. The best are at Sosua, Nagua, and Macao on the Atlantic, that at Macao being many miles long and accessible by three hours' drive (over easily improvable roads) from the capital. Between these three, and along the south coast of Samaná Bay, are many short palm-fringed stretches of white sand and inviting grotto. The best beaches of the Caribbean coastline, none of them large, are between Barahona and Enriquillo on the Cape Beata Peninsula. The shallow wading beaches presently in use, from Boca Chica to San Pedro de Macoris, have nothing to recommend them but accessibility to the capital.

There are three lakes of considerable size in the Republic, all of them in the sea-level depression or "cul-de-sac" running from Barahona to Port-au-Prince, the Haitian capital. Rincon, west of Barahona, is fresh and very shallow, much of it having been diverted into the desert for one of Trujillo's least successful irrigation projects. Limon, the smallest, is brakish. Enriquillo, closest to the border, is thirty-three miles long, below sea level, shallow and predominantly salt. It still contains some fish, turtles, and a few alligators (caimans), and the sight of a flock of pink flamingos silhouetted against its turquoise coves can still be a rare but unforgettable experience. Enriquillo was named for the Indian prince who signed an honorable peace with the Spaniards on Cabritos Island in its center in 1533. Visible above the encircling road, at Las Caritas on the north shore, are coral caves with rudimentary Indian pictographs.

Dominican rivers, in addition to the Yaque del Norte which is 240 miles long and navigable (at least by canoe) from Monte Cristi to Santiago, include: the yellow Yuna, similarly navigable from La Vega in the heart of the country to its swampy delta at the head of Samaná Bay; the Yaque del Sur, flowing from the highest central mountains between San Juan and Constanza into Barahona Bay; and the Ozama and Macoris, deep at their mouths, forming the Caribbean harbors of Santo Domingo and San Pedro de Macoris, respectively.

Four principal mountain ranges parallel each other between the Caribbean and the Atlantic, running more or less from southeast to northwest. Southernmost and shortest is the Baoruco Range, an eastern extension of the towering chain that runs down Haiti's long south peninsula. The Baoruco once gave refuge to Enriquillo and his rebels. It now shelters the depopulated but lovely cul-de-sac with its salt lakes and salt mountain from the southwest winds. Sheltering this valley on the north is the Republic's second range, the Sierra de Neiba, rising at times to six thousand feet and more. The northern slopes of this range form the southern boundary of a wide highland valley that has its narrow neck at Azua and contains the ancient towns of San Juan de la Maguana and Las Matas de Farfan as it widens toward the Haitian border. Forming the northern boundary of these highlands is the third and most important of the Republic's mountain ranges, the Cordillera Central. Running eastward from the wild frontier where it gives source to the Artibonite, Hispaniola's largest river, the Cordillera rises to the 10,300-foot height of Pico Duarte, once called Monte Loma Tina and (briefly) Pico Trujillo, high point of the island—and indeed of the West Indies. In this Dominican "heartland," the Cordillera completely surrounds Constanza Valley and gives source to the Yaque del Norte, one of whose branches, the Jimenoa, forms the Republic's highest falls, unhappily (for nature lovers) thinned out to the practical uses of electric power. Beyond La Vega, the Cordillera breaks up into smaller chains, some running toward the Caribbean and one main spine, the Cordillera Oriental, running almost to Macao Beach at the island's eastern tip. Between the Cordillera Central and the fourth range, the Cordillera Septentrionál, lies the great Cibao Valley, 150 miles long, watered by the Yaque del Norte and, at its eastern end—

the fabulously rich Vega Real—by the Yuna as well. The Cordillera Septentrionál, paralleling the Atlantic coast, and separated from it by a coastal plain of varying width, concludes to the east in a separated extension of low but very rugged hills that fill the entire Samaná Peninsula.

Flora and fauna. Contrary to popular belief, almost none of the familiar fruit-bearing trees and flowering shrubs of Hispaniola and the other Antilles are native to the West Indies.

The short list of undeniable "natives" includes the soursop, star apple, cashew, wild guava, wild pepper, mahogany, logwood, *amapola,* satinwood, frangipani, calabash, royal palm, agave, and longleaf pine. Tobacco, cotton, and kapok are also native.

"Imports" include citrus fruit, transplanted bananas (plantains), and sugar cane from the Canaries; coconut, mango, rose apple, organ cactus, and almond from India and the East Indies; breadfruit from the South Pacific; eucalyptus from Australia; flamboyants, castor-oil plants, and coffee plants from Africa; hibiscus from Asia; bougainvillea from Brazil; poinsettia from Central America; white angel's-trumpet from Peru; cocoa from Mexico; papayas and limes from Venezuela. The Indians themselves are believed to have brought with them from the South American mainland bananas, sweet potatoes, peanuts, and their staple food, the starchy manioc root.

There are few poisonous insects on Hispaniola—the tarantula, scorpion, and centipede are occasionally met with—but the malarial mosquito is still a menace in some of the low-lying coastal towns. There are no poisonous serpents on the island. The iguana and smaller lizards are harmless—and edible. Turtles, small oysters, and every variety of sea fish abound. Sharks make ocean bathing hazardous except behind reefs. The manatee, or sea cow, which led Columbus to report the presence of "mermaids" off Monte Cristi, is extremely rare today. There are some alligators near the mouths of the two Yaques, and in the brakish cul-de-sac lakes. Parrots, pelicans, flamingos, wild pigeons and ducks, swallows, and the sweet-singing nightingale and musician bird (*jilguero*) are native to Hispaniola.

Rodents include the agouti and the hutia or Solenodon (a "missing link" creature discovered in 1907), both very rare since the introduction of the mongoose, which has also decimated the birds. The principal domestic animals—cattle, horses, chickens, sheep, and goats—are not indigenous to Hispaniola. "The population of Azua," said a turn-of-the-century traveler, "is 3,000 humans and 3,000,000 goats."

Minerals. Gold mining, which ceased entirely in 1543 following discovery of the great mines in Mexico and Peru, brought in from $200,000 to $1,000,000 a year between 1502 and 1530. Much of it came from the river sands, but there were pits at Cotui and in the hills behind Santiago and La Vega. An Indian women brought in one nugget so large a suckling pig was served on it. The Indian woman, remarked Padre Las Casas, "was lucky if they gave her a piece of the pig."

Copper, iron, and coal are found in many parts of the Republic. There is some silver and amber. The ten-mile salt mountain near Neiba provides an almost inexhaustible supply of rock salt. Much of the salt used domestically, however, comes from the evaporated sea water caught in traps at Azua, Bani, and Monte Cristi. The largest petroleum deposit so far found is at Azua. There are valuable quarries of limestone, granite, and marble. At present, only a little bauxite and nickel strip mining is being carried on.

Santo Domingo City. As in most Latin American countries, almost all the nation's cultural life and artistic heritage is concentrated in the capital. This is especially true of Santo Domingo since it contains all that remains of the brief but grandiloquent Spanish *Audiencia*. The architecture, much of it in noble ruin, remains. Unlike that of Mexico, it contains no Indian elements, since the Tainos (a less advanced civilization) were exterminated after one generation of Spanish rule. Nor does it contain any innovations in the prevailing Spanish Renaissance style, the architects in many instances having been forced back to earlier patterns in order to comply with needs nonexistent in sixteenth-century Europe. Spanish Colonial architecture, in the words of Erwin Walter Palm, became increasingly "an art in which variation replaced invention and recollection of familiar forms made up for the search for new solutions." No local painting of any quality or originality survives from the colonial period, and in sculpture nothing but a few tombs, the façade decorations of the cathedral, and its wooden Episcopal Chair. The cathedral treasury contains a fine collection of Colonial goldsmith work.

Almost all of the surviving Colonial architecture is concentrated in the small triangle on the west bank of the Ozama River formed by the bend of the stream as it meets the sea. This is Old Santo Domingo, to which the Spaniards moved their capital from the east bank after the hurricane of 1502. Bisected by El Conde, the city's quality shopping thoroughfare, Old Santo Domingo contains the cathedral, the hopelessly "restored" palace of Diego Columbus (incorrectly called "The Alcazar"), the Church of the Mercedes, the House of the Cord, the Ozama Fortress (with its somber *Torre del Homenaje* dungeon, in which Columbus was *not* imprisoned), the ruins of the Franciscan monastery and of the hospital of St. Nicholas of Bari, and the *Puerta del Conde,* a gateway of the ancient wall, from which independence was proclaimed. Space will permit only a brief description of the cathedral here.

Occupying the south side of the *Parque Colón* square, the cathedral is built of golden, warm-glowing coral limestone, which cuts easily but weathers to diamond hardness. The cornerstone of the present structure (which replaced two earlier ones) was laid in 1521, though the magnificent plateresque façade, which faces west, was not completed until 1540. The first architect was Louis de Moya; but the superintendent of its construction was the first resident bishop, Alessandro Geraldini, a Renaissance scholar-poet and friend of the Medici Pope Leo X, patron of Raphael and Michelangelo. The bronze evangelists which once occupied the four flat niches to left and right of the coffered twin gates were presumably lost during Sir Francis Drake's sack of the capital in 1586. One of Drake's cannon balls is still lodged in the tile roof.

The thirty-three-foot-wide columned nave, with flanking aisles almost as high and noble rib vaulting, is presently defaced at the entrance by an ugly "tomb" for Columbus, built in the late nineteenth century following the discovery (1877) of the great explorer's bones in a chancel crypt to the left of the altar. The polychrome and gilded Baroque high altar with spiral columns dates from 1684. The Episcopal Chair is the earliest piece of mahogany furniture in existence and a fine example of sixteenth-century wood carving.

Notable post-Colonial buildings in the capital include the arcaded Old Senate Building on the *Parque Colón,* the only structure known to have been erected by the Haitians during their unproductive two decades of occupation; the executive *Palacio Nacional,* a pseudo High Renaissance palace which was the first and least offensive of Trujillo's public buildings; the *Bellas Artes* and University City buildings and the Model Market, and the Jaragua, Embajador, and Hispaniola Hotels, all likewise built in the Trujillo period.

The National Museum is located in one of the two-story modern buildings in the *Feria* (fairgrounds). The ground floor contained (1963) a very inadequate collection of Arawak (Taino) pieces, few of them identified. Some of the relief-sculpture and figurines on heart-shaped amphora or phallic pestles are surprisingly sophisticated, comparing favorably with Mescal and Toltec artifacts from Mexico. The divided central staircase is embellished with a gay, stylized mural of Indians by Clara Ledesma. The chambers to which it leads contain collections of varying interest: stained plaster casts by Abelardo Rodríguez Urdanata, *ca.* 1900; Spanish bells, several from an old church in Moca; a massive table on which the constitution of 1844 was signed at San Cristobal; souvenirs of Duarte and the other Trinitarios; the inevitable mural by Vela Zanetti, this one a neo-Cubist interpretation of the conquest with Trujillo overtones.

By far the best local collection of pre-Columbian art—some day to be given to the National Museum—is that of Emile de Boyrie Moya, former director of the Dominican Institute of Archaeological Investigation at the university. Its chief glory—and his own discovery—is the group of several hundred orange travertine ceremonial heads found in the caves of Los Paredones behind Boca Chica, and made some time between the "shell culture" of two thousand years ago and the Taino period. Dr. de Boyrie's collection also includes a notable array of paintings and sculpture by contemporary Dominican artists—Paul Giudicelli, Dario Suro, Antonio Prats-Ventos, Jaime Colson, Gilberto Hernández Ortega, and others.

The zoo on Avenida Bolivar contains specimens of all the animals native to Hispaniola—collected on Trujillo's orders by Emile de Boyrie Moya—as well as an assortment of camels, rhinoceroses, lions, bear, ostriches, African birds and mandrils, and a cage of long-haired monkeys that dive into their moat enclosure for peanuts. On weekends and holidays huge crowds pour through the botanical gardens and natural dry grottoes, some attracted perhaps by the Ferris wheels and speedways in the amusement area to the rear.

Eastward to Higüey. Crossing the Ozama on the suspension bridge once named for Trujillo's youngest son, Radhames, the road eastward passes one of the great natural attractions on the island. Only a few kilometers out, and easily missed on the right-hand side, is a sign pointing to *Tres Ojos* (Three Eyes), a complex of subterranean volcanic caverns connected with the undercut sea wall. Rough concrete steps lead down to three pools. The vault-like roofs of all three are festooned with ferns, rope-like lianas, and the nests of innumerable bats. Stalactites and stalagmites enhance this eerie beauty where shafts of sunlight from the limestone roof occasionally dazzle the darkness. The first pool is salt water of a perfect aquamarine transparency. The water in the second and smallest is sulphurous but not hot. The third and largest is of fresh water and has a very strong and dangerous current. The water is being sucked into a tunnel from which, past the vortex, a dry passage some fifty yards long leads to a large, hot sulphur lake, the smoke from which may be seen rising through various openings concealed in the brush above. The first pool provides unusual opportunities for swimming and diving.

Continuing on the highway, past the fishing village of La Caleta, and the Punta Caucedo International Airport (fifteen miles from the capital) is *Boca Chica,* with a small tourist hotel, the Hamaca, on the beach, and many luxurious residences, once the property of the Trujillos and their entourage, nearby. A dirt road leads along the coast to smaller beach settlements, Guayacanes and Juan Dolio. The main road, further inland, leads to San Pedro de Macoris, seventy-five kilometers from the capital.

In the early years of this century, *San Pedro de Macoris* enjoyed great prosperity. It had become the first port and a cultural center of the Republic. Most Dominican sugar passed through its custom house and docks. It had the first telephones, the first electricity, the first concrete buildings in the country. Jenny Lind and Caruso sang in its opera house. Today San Pedro is almost a ghost town. The famous sugar mills inland—Porvenír, Consuelo, Sante Fé, Angelina, Cristoforo Colón, Quisqueya—still grind sugar, but most of it is exported via Santo Domingo. In the thirties, Trujillo decided to concentrate shipping in his show place, the capital. Only the rickety horse-drawn carriages with their brass lamps and intricately chased leather remain to remind one of the provincial splendor that was San Pedro de Macoris, "The Little Paris of the Caribbean." Its present population of twenty-three thousand is in part bilingual—English having been the language of most of the West Indians who came in to cut the cane—but there is a strong contingent of Creole speaking Haitians still (complete with voodoo) and a scattering of Arabs, Lebanese, Italians, and Chinese as well.

From San Pedro the road runs thirty-nine kilometers due north, through flat but beautiful country dotted with innumerable nub-like green hills, to *Hato Mayor*. A poor town of eight thousand inhabitants in the heart of the cattle country, Hato Mayor was once the center of "gavillero" resistance to the American Marine occupation. The town sees little of the four big absentee landlords whose estates completely surround it and whose overseers, one is told, go armed to keep the land-poor townsmen from "squatting." Cowboys are paid eighty-five cents a day, with sometimes a shack to live in. The town's one millionaire is a lumberyard owner, lumber currently bringing twenty-three cents a square foot and being plentiful in the wild hills to the north of the town. The town's small hotel bears the picturesque name *"Asia del Este."* A poor road continues north to Sabana de la Mar on Samaná Bay, where an occasional "ferry" may be obtained to the town of Samaná on the far side. The main highway runs twenty-four kilometers due east to Seibo.

Seibo, or El Seybo, or Santa Cruz del Seybo, is the capital of Seibo province. Founded in 1502 by the conquistador, Juan de Esquivál, it became the country seat of General Pedro Santana, the foundations of whose home, "El Prado," are to be found ten kilometers southwest of the town on land now belonging to the American Central Romana Corporation. Seibo was also the site of the battle of Palo Hincado where Juan Sánchez Ramírez defeated the Napoleonic invaders in 1808. The town has a remarkable little Catholic church, its walls covered with Arabic tiles each one of which bears the inscription, "There is but one God, and Mohamet is his prophet."

Twelve kilometers to the southeast the road branches, a right fork leading thirty-eight kilometers south to La Romana, a left fork thirty-one kilometers east to Higüey.

La Romana, a small and comparatively new town on the south coast, is dwarfed by Central Romana, a very large sugar mill. A subsidiary of the American-owned South Porto Rico Sugar Company, it owns, in addition to mills and cane lands, thousands of acres of the Republic's best cattle land and thousands of head of cattle. In

1963 it had twenty-two thousand employees. A sight of the isolated, clannish American executives' community, with its mile of seaside bungalows smothered in vines and flowers—each with fine lawn, sprinkler system, private gardener, iron gate, and barbed wire— makes one understand why Trujillo's struggle to consolidate the smaller American sugar companies into a single *larger* native combine was one of his more popular undertakings. La Romana has a splendid natural harbor but no beach.

Higüey, with perhaps ten thousand population, is the easternmost town in the Republic. It was founded by Ponce de León, and while nothing of its colonial grandeur remains, it is an attractive place with its one-story wooden houses, deep overhangs, long latched doors with jigsaw transoms in a marvelous variety of pastel colors. Two of Higüey's churches are dedicated to the Virgin of La Altagracia, whose "miracle" took place here in the sixteenth century. The old church, modest and homely, dates from 1630. The new church, still a-building (though in 1963 the pace had slowed down to two stone chippers laboriously "antiquing" the smooth concrete piers) is another multimillion-dollar showpiece put together by those two great architects, Henry Gazón Bona and Trujillo. This one, a series of mammoth dirigible-hangar arches of reinforced concrete, looks like some kind of a spaceship conceived by two small boys with no taste but unlimited resources. It is surrounded by a forest of toadstool-like projections that might be thought to symbolize the evil that sprouts from the police state, but which are actually intended to shelter the twenty thousand pilgrims who come to Higüey annually to celebrate the miracle. Inside, one can easily forget both the building's inappropriateness in the landscape and the brutal offense of its cost; the scale is impressive, the soaring concrete vault silhouettes well where the arches (120 and 250 feet high) superimpose at either end. Even Vela Zanetti's pseudo-Byzantine mosaic murals, tucked away unobtrusively in the trancepts, are pleasant to behold. Across the road from this phenomenon is a small Trujillo-era hotel with the standard chromium-plate balconies, louvered windows, and semiplanted central atrium.

An hour's drive from Higüey over a straight road twenty-nine kilometers northeast is the splendid white-sand beach of *Macao,* many miles long, and protected by a coral reef about half a mile out.

South of Higüey, off the southeast tip of Hispaniola, lies flat, twenty-five-kilometer-long *Saona Island,* once controlled by the Jesuits and very fertile, now uninhabited and barren.

Westward to Barahona. Just beyond the Cattle Coliseum on the four-lane highway to San Cristobal is the spot where Trujillo met his end. The family, in the first months following the assassination, erected their kind of monument on the north side of the road. Nothing remains of it but the concrete base. Those who suffered erected a memorial to the occasion on the south side, with the premise that any mention of the tyrant would be an indecency. The result is one of the most simple and moving of monuments. A bronze strip, tilted to eye level, on a concrete base, bears the legend: "Gloria a la gesta libertadora del 30 de mayo."

About twelve kilometers from the city, on a branch road out of Haina Arriba, site of the huge Rio Haina sugar mills and boat basin, are the gates of *Hacienda Engombe,* once the five thousand acre estate of Hector Trujillo, now the property of the autonomous university. Located on a bend of the Haina River, the estate contains the most extensive Colonial ruins in Hispaniola outside of Old Santo Domingo. Here, at a place called Buenaventura, a sugar magnate of the early sixteenth century (quite possibly the *first* sugar magnate) built for the ages and very nearly made it. The principal buildings of rough-hewn travertine are still discernible: a domed chapel; a large central structure two stories high, with one of its façades (arches and columns) fallen neatly to the ground, surely in an earth tremor; and a long, roofless structure with gun ports that must have been the arsenal. A ditch (defensive moat?) separates these buildings from a smaller group, one shaped like a cross that could have been the powder magazine. The situation, on a bluff overlooking the gently flowing river, is idyllic.

Returning to the highway, the next point of interest is *San Cristobal,* just thirty kilometers from the capital. Eventually the *autopista* will connect with a suspension bridge (already built) over the Nigua River. A small town at the time of Trujillo's birth, known only as the site of the first Dominican Constitutional Convention, San Cristobal was embellished by the Dictator with many imposing squares, parks, and public buildings. In addition to "El Cerro" (see chapter IX), the cathedral, music auditorium, luxuriously appointed hotel, and glass bottling works are noteworthy. Vela Zanetti's frescoes, covering the interior walls and dome of the cathedral, were painted in 1949, and for sheer quantity and speed of execution (four months at $4,000 a month, according to Henry Gazón Bona, the cathedral's architect) must hold some kind of a record. Trujillo's "La Caoba" mansion is a few minutes' drive out of San Cristobal, near the entrance to his vast *Fundación* estate. The nearby spring, La Toma, source of the Nigua and of San Cristobal's water supply, is charmingly situated in a stand of one hundred foot high *ceiba* and dense groves of bamboo.

Thirty-six kilometers beyond San Cristobal is the somewhat larger but less modernized town of *Baní,* birthplace of Maximo Gomez, President Billini, and Father F. X. Billini, a revered philanthropist.

Azua, fifty-five kilometers beyond Baní, is not situated on the bay of the same name, but a little inland. The ports which serve it—Puerto Viejo, Monte Rio, and El Puerto de Azua—attract *aficionados* of swordfishing and skin-diving. Founded in 1504 by Diego Velásquez (soon to become the conqueror of Cuba) and for some years the home of Cortés, Balboa, and Pizarro, Azua in less adventurous times achieved notoriety as the birthplace and base of operations of Buenaventura Baez. Azua's petroleum is not presently being tapped but reputedly is still available in considerable quantities. The town itself, with an attractive yellow church and flamboyant cemetery (on the highway continuing west) is worth visiting.

Most of the eighty kilometers of good road separating Azua from *Barahona* traverses bleak mountains and desert and affords no view of the Caribbean. Barahona itself is a busy port, with sugar mills, salt and gypsum works, and a military airport. The Hotel Guarocuya, built by Trujillo with typical disregard of several adequate beach sites a few thousand yards south, is flanked by factories and docks, its sea front polluted by bagasse and other waste products that float by the cocktail terrace. Even so, as a base for a trip around Lakes Rincon and Enriquillo, which can be made in a day, and for another trip to some of the fine beaches further down the coast—Juan Esteban, La Ciénega, San Rafael, Paraiso, and Enriquillo—a visit to the Guarocuya is recommended. The road to these beaches continues on, deteriorating as it goes, to Cabo Rojo, where Alcoa ships out its bauxite, and finally to Pedernales on the Haitian sea frontier.

Three quarters of the way back to Azua from Barahona, the road forks left and ascends sixty-eight kilometers through fairly high mountains to *San Juan de la Maguana,* ancient capital of San Juan province. This was once the kingdom of the *cacique* Caonabo, and a circle of great stones on a level plain near the town ("El Corral de los Indios") is still to be seen. San Juan also has a modern hotel of its own, the Maguana, and a small airport. A bronze statue of the Trinitario, Francisco del Rosario Sánchez, a native son, stands in the center of the gracious tree-shaded square. By a dry stream bed on the way out of the town hangs one of the world's more improbable signs; it reads (in English): "No Nude Bathing."

Beyond San Juan the road continues thirty-three kilometers to Las Matas and twenty-one kilometers still further west to Elias Piña on the Haitian border.

North to the Cibao. The original Duarte highway connecting the capital with Santiago and the other cities of the Cibao was begun under the American occupation. The new *autopista* was completed (or almost completed) by Trujillo. Hitherto the internal history of the country was determined by the fact that communication between its commercial-political hub and its "bread-basket" was extremely difficult. In 1873 the American traveler, Samuel Hazzard, noted that when one proposed crossing the country by land, "people seemed to think that man must be either crazy or that he expected to derive some mysterious benefit from such a trip; and we were mysteriously told that the trip was almost an impossibility and accompanied with unheard of dangers and risks." As late as 1914 another American traveler, A. Hyatt Verrill, described the road as "mostly a narrow bridle path with rocks, sweeping lianas and hipdeep mud in rainy season." There was a tradition, he added, that a carriage had once been driven from La Vega to Monte Cristi, but he took no stock in it. Today the 131 kilometers from Santo Domingo to La Vega can be driven in well under two hours, and the other principal cities of the Cibao—San Francisco de Macoris, Moca, and Santiago—are easily reached from La Vega.

La Vega, historically, is the most interesting of the four, having within its environs both the ruins of Columbus' original settlement, Concepción de la Vega, and the Santo Cerro (Holy Mountain) from which Columbus watched his armored men and bloodhounds massacre (with divine intervention?) the helpless Indians. The ruins of Columbus' brick fortress and church lie eight kilometers north of La Vega between the old and new roads to Santiago. The circular fort is astonishing for its smallness, being not more than twenty feet in diameter on the inside, with a narrow entrance and six triangular chambers, each leading to a gun port shaped like an inverted keyhole in the six foot thick walls. What is left of the church is perhaps twelve to fifteen feet high. Both structures sank several feet into the ground following one of the sixteenth-century earthquakes. The Santo Cerro has nothing to show for its colonial past but a hole in the floor of the Church of the Virgin of Las Mercedes. Here, according to local tradition, was where the Admiral planted his cross during the battle of March 25, 1494. The church itself dates from 1860, and the nearby Colegio Fantino from 1940. Under the huge laurel tree in the college patio one may obtain a breath-taking view of the *Vega Real,* most resplendent in January when as far as the eye can see thousands of coffee-shading *amapola* trees in full bloom provide coral-pink islands in the deep green ocean of verdure stretching to the horizon.

San Francisco de Macoris, forty-seven kilometers east of La Vega across this plain on secondary paved roads, was described by Verrill as a "white" town noted for the number of its inhabitants of "pure Spanish descent" and celebrated for the beauty of its women. Today, despite its situation in the Vega Real with all that fabled fifteen foot deep loam, San Francisco gives every appearance of being a very poor town; its most notable sight—a group of decapitated statues once intended to glorify the Benefactor—could be taken to symbolize its victimization at the hands of absentee landlords.

A bad road continues eastward by devious stages to the Samaná Peninsula. The towns of Sánchez and Samaná may also be reached, however, by way of the La Vega-Sánchez narrow-gauge railway—a delightful trip through jungle and swampland—or directly from the capital by plane or boat. Almost all of the country around Nagua to the north, or east along the south shore of Samaná Bay, is virgin territory: densely wooded, full of caves and cascades, and roadless.

Just north of La Vega a fork in the old road to Santiago branches south to *Buena Vista, Jarabacoa,* and *Constanza* on the edge of the Cordillera Central. Two of Trujillo's arbitrarily situated resort hotels service this mountain vacation land, the Montaña at Buena Vista and the Nueva Suiza near Constanza. The first is nineteen kilometers from La Vega, the second fifty-nine kilometers further on. Except in the rainy season, the dirt road to Constanza is excellent, and the view, especially around Jarabacoa, is superb. Pico Duarte may be seen in the distance, and a short side trip to the falls of the Jimenoa, which must be approached on foot through a boulder-strewn stream bed, is rewarding. Why the Nueva Suiza was built on the bottom slope of the cup of high mountains surrounding Constanza and cutting off all view of the peaks to the west is a mystery that probably only Trujillo himself could have answered. Why the delightful outdoor swimming pool is two kilometers from the hotel is another mystery. Here the water cascades from a natural mountain stream over rocks and is then caught in a *piscina* complete with high board, children's wading pool, Swiss chalet, and jukebox.

Moca, twenty-one kilometers due north of La Vega on the Duarte highway, was a prosperous town even when Samuel Hazzard visited it and was offered a home with a thousand acres of land cleared for cane, coffee, cotton, cocoa, and fruit for $1,000—"a grand speculation with a stable government assured." Here, near the old "Bolivia" school, Heureaux's assassination brought one period of "stable government" to an end. In another such period, the Sacred Heart of Jesus Cathedral was built with a subvention of $100,000 from Trujillo himself and $500,000 collected (mostly in pennies) from Moca's fifteen thousand inhabitants. The architect, Humberto Ruiz Castillo, was a Dominican, but everything else, including the poor quality stained glass from Turin and the elaborate mosaics, was imported from Europe.

Santiago, the Republic's second city (population one hundred thousand) is forty-four kilometers northwest of La Vega on the main highway. It is also on the Yaque del Norte River and is connected by road and railway (Trujillo removed the tracks to build his sugar mills) with Puerto Plata, sixty-one kilometers north, the Republic's principal Atlantic port. Originally settled in 1504 by thirty Spanish gentlemen (Santiago de los Caballeros is the full name), Santiago, between devastating earthquakes and home-grown insurrections, has had a turbulent history, although the clean, prosperous, and conservative city gives little indication of it. The tree shaded squares with their horse-drawn carriages and solidly built homes seem impervious to politics or personal megalomania. Actually, however, the city lost an architectural treasure in the fifties when Trujillo's mania for "modernization" led to the destruction of some of the finest buildings in the city. The Dictator's unsightly "Peace" monument, dominating one side of the city, and a $4,000,000 suspension bridge over the Yaque that leads nowhere will long remain. Close to the monument a Trujillo-built luxury hotel, the Matum, is the scene of Saturday night dances that attract hundreds of elegantly dressed middle-class couples from all over the Cibao.

The road over the mountains to *Puerto Plata* with its dozens of hairpin turns and thousands of potholes (1963) was designed for the Marines and became a $200,000 political bonanza of Vásquez' times. The abandoned railway, which must have counted its waste in the millions, was started by Westendorp and Company in 1893 and continued by the San Domingo Improvement Company of New York. Rising two thousand feet on steep grades, its trains plunged through the one-thousand-foot Cumbre tunnel to Santiago. The automobile road, for all its difficulties, runs through some of the lushest countryside imaginable, all cultivated, with splendid coffee and banana *fincas* on either side. Eleven kilometers short of Puerta Plata, a right fork of the road leads to Sosua, and, further on, to Nagua, Sánchez, and Samaná. Two kilometers short of the city another right fork leads to "Long Beach" with its Hotel Bambú and *Balneario Colón.* This installation is on a naturally lovely beach, not wide but white-sanded and extending to Sosua and beyond. It is disfigured by two crumbling concrete diving platforms, one bearing the ubiquitous "Brugal" rum sign. There is also a ramshackle casino with some interesting murals by a self-taught artist, depicting the Indians and their gods being displaced by Columbus and his. The town itself is attractively situated overlooking the bay and has warehouses along the grassy waterfront faded to haunting pastel shades.

From Puerto Plata west along the coast via Luperón to the ruins of Columbus' original settlement, *La Isabela,* is little more than sixty kilometers, but the roads are ruinous, and the ruins are little more than a few stones buried in weeds. Everything about the site, which Columbus' doctor described in 1494 as having "a very good harbor and fine fishing," was wrong. There was no harbor at all;

the fishing is the same all along the coast; and since the mouth of the Bajabonico is two kilometers southwest, there was not even drinking water. Gold, and gold alone, dictated the decision not to move on to Puerto Plata. The Indians insisted that this was the gateway to the treasures of the "Cibao," and Columbus, always the wishful thinker, confused the word with Cipango (Japan) and found a double motive for making a major mistake.

The main highway from Santiago to Monte Cristi bypasses the river ports Valverde and Guayubín. These are the centers of the banana plantations for which the giant American United Fruit Company now acts only as buyer and shipper (via Manzanillo Bay to the west). In 1963 agents of United were buying five to six million stems annually from the twenty thousand acres under cultivation, helping with loans for necessary irrigation—the twenty-five inches of rainfall are nowhere near the one hundred inches required—and providing helicopters for spraying. From Guayubín, a good branch road forks south to Santiago Rodríguez, capital of the province of the same name and a town full of bustling enterprise. A road from Santiago Rodriguez runs west forty-one kilometers to *Dajabón,* frontier gateway to northern Haiti across the Massacre River and scene of the worst atrocities during Trujillo's 1937 bloodbath. From Dajabón, the so-called International highway leads south along the border, through Loma de Cabrera, Restauración, and Bánica on the Artibonite, to Elías Piña. At intervals along its mountainous course, guardhouses, with curiously medieval crenelated towers, survey the populous, dark lands to the west.

Monte Cristi, terminus of the highway from Santiago, is situated a little off the coast, midway between camel-backed El Morro and the mouth of the Yaque del Norte. The country roundabout is desert dry, a condition symbolized by the picturesque salt traps. "For months and months," wrote Hazzard in 1873, "it never rains a drop here, and two years ago for one whole year it never rained at all." The beach is narrower than Puerto Plata's and the water not nearly so deep. When the wind "blows the wrong way" the water is black with seaweed and debris. A beach house, once the "Club Ramfis," was being turned into the "Hotel Atlantic" in 1963. Meanwhile the "El Morro" in town, a sedate verandaed establishment painted canary yellow, was doing nicely. Monte Cristi will never make it as a resort, but as a place to visit, explore, and enjoy, there is much to recommend it.

Selected Bibliography

COLONIAL PERIOD

Las Casas, Bartolomé de. *Historia de las Indias*. Madrid, 1875-76.
Moreau de St.-Mery, M. L. E. *A Topographical and Political Description of the Spanish Part of Santo-Domingo*. Translated by William Cobbett. Philadelphia, 1796.
Morison, Samuel Eliot. *Admiral of the Ocean Sea. A Life of Christopher Columbus*. Boston, 1942.

Other Sources

Galván, Manuel de Jesús. *The Cross and the Sword* ("Enriquillo"). Translated by Robert Graves with a Foreword by Max Henríquez Ureña. Bloomington, Ind., 1954.
Labat, Le R. Père. *Nouveau voyage aux îles de l'Amérique*. 8 vols. Paris, 1742.
Rouse, Irving. *The West Indies: The Ciboney, the Carib, the Arawak*. Bureau of American Ethnology, bulletin 143.
Schoenrich, Otto. *Santo Domingo: A Country with a Future* (includes "Historical Sketch" up to 1918). New York, 1918.

HAITIAN INVASIONS AND OCCUPATION

Edwards, Bryan. *An Historical Survey of the Island of Saint Domingo, etc.* London, 1796.
Korngold, Ralph. *Citizen Toussaint*. Boston, 1944.
Lacroix, Pamphile de. *Memoires pour servir à l'histoire de la révolution de Saint-Domingue*. 2 vols. Paris, 1820.
Lepelletier de St.-Rémy, R. *Saint-Domingue. Étude et solution de la question Haïtienne*. Paris, 1846.
Leyburn, James G. *The Haitian People*. New Haven, 1941.
Rodman, Selden. *Haiti: The Black Republic*. New York, 1954.

Schoelcher, V. *Colonies étrangères et Haiti: Resultats de l'émancipation anglaise.* 2 vols. Paris, 1842.

Stoddard, T. Lothrop. *The French Revolution in San Domingo.* New York, 1914.

Wimpffen, Baron de. *A Voyage to Santo Domingo in the Years 1788, 1789, and 1790.* London, 1797.

INDEPENDENCE

Balaguer, Joaquín. *El Cristo de la Libertad. Vida de Juan Pablo Duarte.* Buenos Aires, 1958.

Henríquez y Carvajal, Federico. *Duarte: Proceres, heroes y martires de la independencia.* Ciudad Trujillo, 1944.

Demorizi, Emilio Rodríguez. *Juan Isidro Pérez: El ilustre loco.* Ciudad Trujillo, 1944.

Veloz, Enrique Patin. *El sentido masonico de la vida y la obra de Duarte.* Ciudad Trujillo, 1956.

THE NINETEENTH CENTURY

Welles, Sumner. *Naboth's Vineyard: The Dominican Republic 1844-1924.* 2 vols. New York, 1928.

Other Sources

Espaillat, Ulises Francisco. *Escritos.* 2 vols. Santo Domingo, 1962.

————. *Ideas de dien patrio.* Selección de Emilio Rodriguez Demorizi. Santo Domingo, 1962.

Hazzard, Samuel. *Santo Domingo Past and Present, with a Glance at Hayti.* New York, 1873.

Hearings on Haiti and Santo Domingo. Sixty-seventh Congress Report (Senate). Washington, D.C., 1922.

Heinl, Robert Debs, Jr. *Soldiers of the Sea. The United States Marine Corps, 1775-1962.* Annapolis, Md., 1962.

Kelsey, Carl. *The American Intervention in Haiti and the Dominican Republic.* American Academy of Political and Social Science, 1921.

Luperón, Gregorio. *Notas autobiográficas y apuntes históricos sobre la República Dominicana.* 3 vols. Madrid, n.d.

Meriño, Fernando A. de. *Elementos de geografía física, política é histórica de la República Dominicano.* Santo Domingo, 1898.

Ober, F. A. "The Late President of Santo Domingo," *Independent,* XXXI (Oct. 19, 1899), 2821-24.

Verrill, A. Hyatt. *Porto Rico Past and Present and San Domingo of Today.* New York, 1914.

Willis, Francis L. "Heureaux and His Island Republic," *National Magazine,* X (September, 1899), 563-71.

TRUJILLO AND AFTER

Baciu, Stefan. *Juan Bosch: Del exilio a la presidencia.* Santo Domingo, 1963.

Besault, Lawrence de. *President Trujillo: His Work and the Dominican Republic.* Printed abroad for the government, 1936.

Bosch, Juan. *Trujillo: Causas de una tiranía sin ejemplo.* Caracas, 1959.

Clark, Gerald. *The Coming Explosion in Latin America.* New York, 1963.

Dominican Republic (two pamphlets). Pan-American Union, Washington, D.C., 1951, 1958.

Diaz-Balart, Rafael L. *Antitrujillismo y solidaridad. Extracto de un libro en preparación* (Notes on Cayo Confites Expedition). New York, 1959.

Espaillat, Arturo R. *Trujillo: The Last of the Caesars.* Chicago, 1963.

Galíndez, Jesús de. *La era de Trujillo.* Santiago de Chile, 1956.

Gazón Bona, Henry. *La arquitectura dominicana en la era de Trujillo.* Ciudad Trujillo, 1949.

Gonzales-Blanco, Pedro. *Trujillo: La restauración de un pueblo.* Mexico, 1946.

Gall, Norman. "Anatomy of a Coup: The Fall of Juan Bosch," *Nation* (Oct. 26, 1963).

———. "How Trujillo Died," *New Republic* (April, 1963).

Harding, Bertita. *The Land Columbus Loved, the Dominican Republic.* New York, 1949.

Hicks, Albert C. *Blood in the Streets: The Life and Rule of Trujillo.* New York, 1946.

Ornes, Germán E. *Trujillo: Little Caesar of the Caribbean.* New York, 1958.

Szulc, Tad. "Trujillo's Legacy: A Democratic Vacuum," New York *Times* Sunday Magazine, Sept. 2, 1962.

———. "After Trujillo, a Reformer with a Mission," New York *Times* Sunday Magazine, Sept. 8, 1963.

Times Profile. "Dedicated Dominican: Juan Bosch," New York *Times,* May 4, 1963.

Trujillo, Rafael Leonidas. *The Basic Policies of a Regime.* Ciudad Trujillo, 1960.

———. *The Evolution of Democracy in Santo Domingo.* Ciudad Trujillo, 1950, 1955.

Vicini, José D. *La Isla del Azúcar.* Ciudad Trujillo, 1957.

World Trade Information Service. *Basic Data on the Economy of the Dominican Republic.* Washington, D.C., 1957.

Walker, Stanley. *Journey Toward the Sunlight.* New York, 1947.

Other Sources

Rodman, Selden. Extracts from *Journal,* Vol. XVI. Including interviews with Juan Bosch, Buenaventura Sánchez, Donald Reid Cabral, Viriato A. Fiallo, Generals Antonio Imbert Barrera, and others. Unpublished.

GENERAL

Balaguer, Joaquín. *Historia de la literatura dominicana.* Ciudad Trujillo, 1958.

Boyrie Moya, Emile de. *Las piezas arqueológicas, de material travertinico, de las "Cuevas de los Paredones" (Caleta II) Republica Dominicana.* Ciudad Trujillo, 1952.

Cochrane, Doris M. *The Herpatology of Hispaniola.* Washington, D.C., 1941.

Coopersmith, J. M. *Music and Musicians of the Dominican Republic.* Washington, D.C., 1949.

Hostos, Eugenio María de. *Moral social.* Santo Domingo, 1962.

Mañach, Jorge. *Martí: Apostle of Freedom.* New York, 1950.

Palm, Erwin Walter. *Los Monumentos arquitectónicos de la Española.* 2 vols. Ciudad Trujillo, 1955.

————. *The Pocket Guide to Ciudad Trujillo.* Ciudad Trujillo, 1951.

Wetmore, Alexander, and Bradshaw H. Swales. *The Birds of Haiti and the Dominican Republic.* Washington, D.C., 1931.

Index